KW-362-869

Contents

Foreword

This year, 1976, the Audience Research Department celebrates its 40th Anniversary. An article charting the development of listening and viewing in Britain over this period opens this third Annual Review. Apart from this, the pattern established by the two preceding Annual Reviews has been followed. First comes a note on the amount of viewing recorded during the year, with audiences examined in socio-economic group terms. This is followed by one on the amount of listening. Then come summarised reactions to a broad selection of programmes, first television and then radio, and finally a few more extended reports on some of the special enquiries conducted during the year. Notable amongst these is the study of the contribution made by broadcasting during the campaign leading up to the EEC Referendum.

The results obtained in the enquiries undertaken by the Audience Research Department are normally kept confidential, at least until some time has elapsed since the studies were made, but the *methods* used have always been open to enquiry. Indeed, they have been the subject of many articles in various journals. A new edition of the Department's booklet describing them in detail has recently been printed. It is entitled 'BBC Audience Research in the United Kingdom: Methods and Services' and copies are available on request from the Department.

Included in the booklet is a note explaining why our audience size estimates may appear to be at variance with those produced by JICTAR. These apparent discrepancies – which arise largely because we and JICTAR seek to measure different things – have been a long-standing cause for concern, but the search for a single audience measurement system that would provide for the differing needs of the various parties has so far been abortive. The possibility of collaboration in this field was once again explored in considerable detail during 1975/6, but the only method that seemed likely to satisfy everyone's needs proved to have serious snags. The simple facts are (i) that commercial television interests need information about an individual's viewing for several months, so that the 'reach' of a campaign can be studied; this, in research terms, implies using a ‘diary’ method, in which people keep records of their viewing; and (ii) that the BBC needs information about listening as well as viewing; a diary including radio as well as television programmes is complicated to produce and demanding to fill in, whereas the personal interview method can cope with both radio and television without strain. Discussions are continuing in the hope of finding an acceptable ‘common data source’, but the earliest that any such system could start operating would be July 1979.

Forty Years of Listening and Viewing in Britain

It was on 1 October 1936 that Listener Research (as it was then known) formally began in the BBC.* Very early in its existence it was realised that one of the most valuable services that the infant department could supply would be the provision of estimates of audience size. A recommendation to institute regular audience size measurement was made, and blessed, in June 1937, but it was to be two-and-a-half years more before a continuous service could be set up. The intervening time was a period of experiment, of consideration of alternative methods and examination of experience in America, where regular audience measurement (by telephone surveys) was already under way.

It was experiments in 1938 that yielded the first 'hard' information about listening in Britain; though in view of the fact that the data were derived from a volunteer panel, there must be some reservations about the reliability of the findings. With this proviso, the profile of listening in 1938 would seem to have had as its peaks the 6.00 p.m. News (not the 9.00 p.m., which competed with regional programmes) and a range of entertainment programmes that included *Monday Night at Seven*, *In Town Tonight*, *Band Waggon* and some early *Scrapbook* programmes. All these were heard by seven or eight times as many as listened to serious programmes such as talks and symphony concerts.

Nothing reliable is known about listening earlier in the '30s. However, confirmation that the broad patterns emerging from the first experiments had existed for at least a year or two came from a special survey, also conducted in 1938, in which people were questioned about their programme likes and dislikes. Their replies can safely be taken to reflect their listening behaviour in the previous year or two, in a rough-and-ready way of course. Of twenty-one different kinds of programmes, 'variety' came top (liked by 93%), followed by cinema organs, military bands, dance music and plays, with chamber music bringing up the rear (8%). The 1938 experimental findings put audiences in very much this order,

* For an account of the history of the Department see *Who's Listening?* by R. J. E. Silvey, George Allen & Unwin Ltd., 1974.

once allowance is made for factors such as timings, and there seems little doubt that results in 1937 and 1936 would have been much the same, had regular surveys been going then. (Incidentally, similar enquiries over the years have revealed a fairly static 'taste picture'. Cinema organs and military bands did not appear on subsequent lists – if they had, their followings would probably have been much smaller – but in general it can be said that the findings have revealed no dramatic changes in the 'liking' for different kinds of broadcast material.)

Three months after the outbreak of war, the regular survey of listening started – the daily Survey that has continued without a break and that still provides the BBC with its estimates of listening and viewing audiences today. Here are the results for the very first day, 3 December 1939.

General Listening Barometer – Week 49 *Confidential*

Return for Sunday, 3 December 1939

Subject to the limitations of sampling, the figures below show the percentage of the whole adult population of Great Britain who listened to each item.

a.m.		%
7.00	News	3·7
7.10	Entr'acte Players	1·6
7.40	BBC Theatre Organ: Frank Newman	4·3
8.00	News	16·9
8.10	Baxendale's (Manchester) Works Band	9·7
8.50	Talk: 'December in the Country'. W. Aspden	4·2
9.00	Harry Engleman's Quintet	6·0
9.25	Service from Lichfield Cathedral	13·5
10.15	BBC Orchestra (Section C) with Mary Hamlin	8·0
11.00	The Tudor Sextet	6·8
11.30	Feature Programme: 'Bound Away'	9·1
12.00	'I Remember': presented by Percy Edgar	9·6
p.m.		
12.40	Great Occasions: 'Marie Curie and the Discovery of Radium'	11·0
1.00	News	39·4
1.10	Busoni Sonata (Violin and Piano)	9·5
1.45	BBC Theatre Organ: Reginald Foort	24·5
2.15	Talk: C. H. Middleton and A. H. Moss	14·5
2.30	Sunday Orchestral Concert from Sadler's Wells	11·0
3.30	Don Felipe and the Cuban Caballeros	13·9
4.00	News	31·2
4.15	'What is Man?' (5) Dr W. R. Matthews	9·3
4.35	Louis Levy and Concert Orchestra	18·5
5.15	Children's Hour	13·8
6.00	News	42·6
6.15	BBC Orchestra (Section B)	10·7
6.50	'Scenes from Pickwick' – 5	14·6
7.25	Fred Hartley Septet and Brian Lawrance	21·2
7.55	Religious Service from the Studio	19·8

p.m.		%
8·40	Week's Good Cause: Rev. Pat McCormick	19·6
8·45	'Making your own Music' – 2, R. Vaughan Williams	11·9
9.00	News	45·6
9.15	'Scrapbook for 1910'	37·1
10.15	'Pictures in the Fire': BBC Military Band	18·9
10.45	Epilogue	9·7
10.55	The Kutcher String Quartet	4·5
11.30	BBC Salon Orchestra	4·1
12.00	News	9·1
	Broadcasts in Welsh	
pm		
5.30	Service in Welsh from Swansea	1·5
6.15	News in Welsh	0·3

GLB/DR 1

Listener Research Section
8.12.39

The listening pattern that continued for the next five years had already been set, the audiences for the 9.00 p.m. News dominating the listening figures at around 50% of the population, with the 6.00 p.m. News attracting around 40% and the 8.00 a.m. News 25%. Apart from the News, it was the light entertainment shows that most people listened to, those with audiences of about 40% including *Henry Hall's Guest Night*, *Garrison Theatre* and *ITMA*. The appetite for the theatre organ is exemplified by the following for Sandy Macpherson's programmes, many of which were heard by at least 25%, as were some early Paul Temple mystery plays. The habit of turning to broadcasting on Christmas Day had already begun, Christmas Day 1939 bringing the first audience of over 60%, when Gracie Fields was heard by an estimated 67·5%.

The Forces Programme began early in 1940, but many evening programmes were broadcast simultaneously on the Home Service and the Forces Programme, notably all the News bulletins. Early successes in the Forces Programme included *Hi, Gang!* and the specially designed *Ack-Ack, Beer-Beer* (for people on lonely anti-aircraft sites) but the Home Service continued to dominate the scene with its well-established ingredients, plus some new regular features such as the Postscripts following the 9.00 p.m. News. Many well-known figures contributed to these talks, but the biggest attraction then, and for a long time afterwards, proved to be J. B. Priestley. Incidentally, it was a J. B. Priestley Postscript that was the subject of the Department's first study of how well, or badly, broadcasts communicate. The report on the study includes . . . 'Of the 240 persons who heard it, only one-sixth said they could recall nothing about it. ("But then you never can pin him down to anything . . ." said a Chelmsford housewife.) Half had a clear memory of it, many giving details; the balance, some recollection, if vague.'

A noteworthy record audience for a day other than Christmas Day was for the 9.00 p.m. News on 14 July, heard by 64·4%. This was 'special' in that it was preceded by a statement by the Prime Minister and included Charles Gardner's running commentary on an aerial battle over the Channel.

New records were set in 1941 and 1942 by the audiences recorded for the series of broadcasts by Winston Churchill, one of which reached 76·9%, whilst two others also topped the 70% mark. News bulletins continued to be listened to avidly, with a whole range of light entertainment shows all attracting large audiences of about 40% (*Happidrome*, *Flanagan and Allen*, *Henry Hall's Guest Night*, *ITMA*, etc.). Amongst the distinguished feature programmes was Louis MacNeice's *Alexander Nevsky* in December 1941, which was heard by 15%, whilst Raymond Gram Swing's *American Commentary* substantially increased its audience from 14% to 21% once the United States entered the War. These years also saw the start of *The Brains Trust* and of the still-running *Desert Island Discs*.

Listening followed much the same pattern as this for the remainder of the War. There were some further speeches by Churchill, heard by 60% or more, whilst General Smuts, Lord Beaverbrook and Mrs Roosevelt all topped the 50% mark. And not far short of it came the Postscript by comedian George Formby. However, it was D-Day that saw a new record established, an estimated 80·3% hearing the 9.00 p.m. announcement. *ITMA* audiences reached new heights towards the end of 1944 at 48%, and there was a piquant confrontation between the Will Hay programme on the Home Service and Bob Hope on the General Forces Programme. The Scottish comedian's audience was three times as big as Hope's! Though light entertainment remained the peak attraction, except for the News, two drama series began to rival the followings of many of the comedy shows. They were *Saturday Night Theatre* and the mystery plays *Appointment with Fear*. These, and the light music series *Grand Hotel*, were heard by some 30%. There was also an eye-catching debate 'Should Party Government Return with Peace?' between Quintin Hogg and Aneurin Bevan, heard by 13%.

1945 saw the War brought to an end, the Prime Minister's 3.00 p.m. announcement on VE-Day being heard by 71·5%. Nine o'clock News audiences had remained at 50% or over *until* VE-Day, but they then fell to 40%, and further still to 35% by the end of the year. Amongst other noteworthy audiences were those for the *Election Speeches* in June 1945, averaging 45% – a tribute to their novelty – and for the fourth performance of the play cycle written for *Children's Hour, The Man Born to be King* (19%, and the largest so far). Old wartime favourites went on attracting listeners right through 1946, but most were being overtaken by the new *Merry-Go-Round, Stand Easy* and *Carol Levis's Discoveries*, with *Ignorance is Bliss* and *Much Binding in the Marsh* not far behind. *Have a Go* started its meteoric career when, after transferring from the North Region to the Light Programme in September 1946, its audience steadily rose to 45% by early 1947 and to an *average* of 54% a year later. This remains a record for a regular light entertainment show, on radio *or* television.

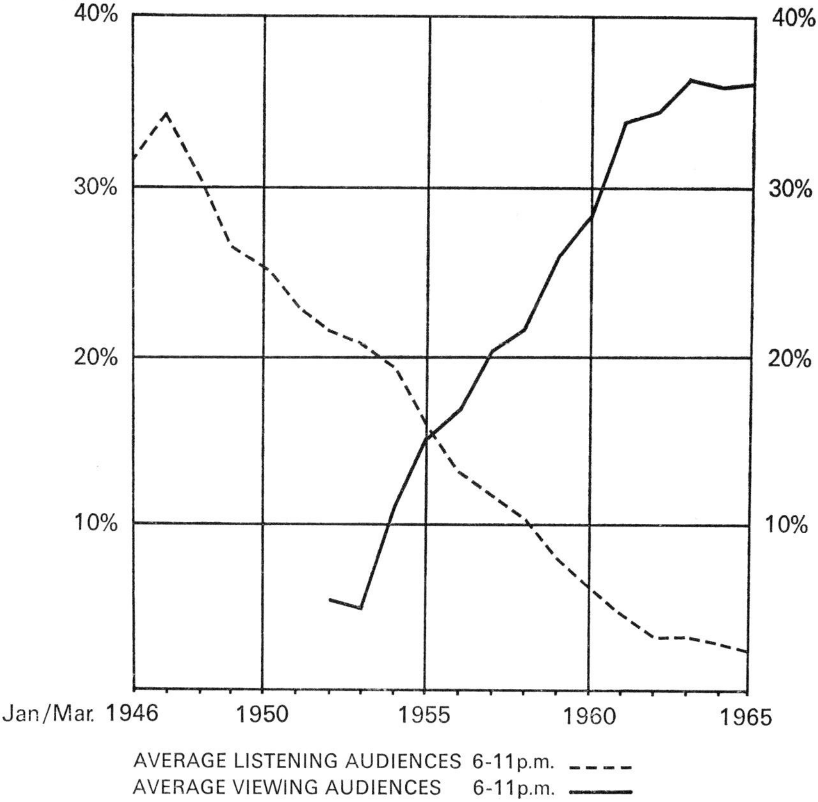

From 1939 to 1945 listening habits were built around News bulletins to such an extent that weekly statistics summarising the amount of listening kept News and announcements of all kinds separate from other programmes. From 1946 onwards 'average audience' figures that *included*

News began to be calculated, for two time bands, 9.00 a.m. to 6.00 p.m. and 6.00 p.m. to 11.00 p.m. The evening period figures given in the chart above show how, in the 1950s, viewing steadily took over from listening.

By 1956 there were more people viewing than listening between 6.00 and 11.00 p.m., and by 1965 evening listening had reached the comparatively low level at which it still remains. It is also notable that 'devoting a lot of time to broadcasting' is not a new phenomenon peculiar to the television age. The *total* amount of time spent listening or viewing between 6.00 and 11.00 p.m. has fluctuated between about 35% in 1947 to about 26% in 1953, with a subsequent rise to about 40% ten years later. This has been the level ever since. (In considering these estimates the restricted television transmission hours during the early 1950s must be borne in mind.)

So, from the exceptionally large radio light entertainment audiences of the late 1940s, the big battalions gradually moved to television. The early television buyers watched practically everything avidly, but this honeymoon period soon passed, and in any event by the end of 1955 viewing had to be shared between the BBC and the newcomer, ITV. Apart from a few months when they were readjusting their viewing habits, viewers with a choice of programmes soon showed a marked preference for ITV – a situation that continued until 1961/2, when the rough parity that has been maintained ever since was finally achieved.

The coming of new services (BBC2 and Local Radio) have not, as yet, appreciably altered the national picture, though in some areas the local stations (BBC or Independent) have, it seems, both boosted total listening and made inroads into the established choice of channels. More about these latest changes will be found in the 'Viewing During the Year' and 'Listening During the Year' sections in this and earlier Annual Reviews.

Review of the year

1 Viewing in the United Kingdom in 1975/6

The rate of growth in the proportion of the population with colour television slowed down sharply in 1975/6, the rise during the year being only from 47% in the first quarter of 1975 to 53% in the first quarter of 1976. This increase of 6% is no more than half as great as the increases in the three preceding years, thus:

Proportion of population of UK with colour television in January/March	%
1971	4·2
1972	10·3
1973	21·1
1974	35·9
1975	47·2
1976	53·8

The virtual pegging of incomes has clearly had a very marked effect on the acquisition of an expensive item such as this. Nearly all the rest of the population have monochrome receivers, all but a few (3·5%) having sets with UHF bands, enabling them to receive all three channels.

There was a little less viewing in 1975/6 than in the preceding twelve months, the weekly averages being 17 hours 24 minutes per head and 17 hours 40 minutes per head respectively. Most of the drop came in the summer months, the 1975 summer not only being a fine one,* but also not being the occasion of a major sporting event, such as the World Cup or the Olympic Games. Besides increasing total viewing, events like these have often given BBC Television a big lead over ITV in the share-of-viewing statistics, but this year a clear lead was achieved by BBC Television without the benefit of any such event, other than the *Winter* Olympics. Taking the year as a whole, BBC1 attracted 47% of all viewing, ITV attracted 45%, and BBC2 the remaining 8%, the pattern being much

* Though not as hot and dry as 1976!

the same in all four quarters. In previous years it has generally been ITV that has taken the biggest share.

The peak audiences of the year were, as usual, recorded for some of the Christmas Day programmes – *Morecambe and Wise, Are You Being Served?, Butch Cassidy and the Sundance Kid* – together with two other regular annual attractions – *Miss World* and the *Royal Variety Performance*. All these were seen by about 50% of the population. This year, however, they were joined by ITV's first showing of the James Bond film *Dr. No*, with two other films – *The Italian Job* and *The Longest Day* – not far behind.

The viewing figures on the day that *Dr. No* was transmitted (28 October) provided another example of how little large audiences generally owe to cross-channel switching. *Dr. No* at 8.00 p.m. drew 9 million more viewers than did the Benny Hill show that preceded it on ITV, whilst at the same time BBC Television's audience fell by 4 million viewers. However, not all of Benny Hill's audience went on to view *Dr. No* (a million did not), nor did all those leaving BBC Television desert it for ITV (another million did not). The bulk of the increase in ITV's audience thus consisted of people who had not been viewing any of the television channels at all before 8.00 p.m. This has almost invariably proved to be the case when similar situations have been analysed in the past.

Statistics presented in previous Annual Reviews have shown how big an influence socio-economic group membership has on channel choice. The numerically small 'A' group generally spends less than one-third of its viewing time with ITV, compared with well over half for the very much more numerous 'C' group. The 'A' group's use of BBC2, though it does not rival their use of the other two channels, is nevertheless twice as big as is the share given to BBC2 by the 'Cs', and so on. In 1975 a different and more detailed analysis was made, which showed the audiences amongst each of the three socio-economic groups series-by-series. The averages for evening series (post 5.45 p.m.) on the three channels turned out to be:

	Average Audiences for Evening Series on		
	BBC1	*BBC2*	*ITV*
	%	%	%
Amongst socio-economic group A	15·2	3·8	8·2
Amongst socio-economic group B	15·3	3·2	12·1
Amongst socio-economic group C	13·4	2·6	19·7

The average audience for BBC1 evening programmes was much the same amongst all three socio-economic groups, the 'middle-class' groups 'A' and 'B' tending to view this channel slightly more than did the Cs'. Even so, there were great variations in the viewing patterns. For twelve of the series studied, the 'Cs' viewed more than did the 'As', an extreme instance being *Lulu*, for which the socio-economic group audiences were respectively 'As' 6%, 'Bs' 19% and 'Cs' 30%. Other series in this group of 'exceptions' were *Bruce Forsyth and the Generation Game*, *Kojak*, *Till Death Us Do Part*, *Sportsnight*, *Top of the Pops*, *The Good Old Days*, *Come Dancing* and two series of films, *The Saturday Movie* and *The Late Film* on Fridays. At the other extreme were twelve series for which the audiences amongst the 'As' were more than half as big again as amongst the 'Cs'. These were mainly 9.00 p.m. News bulletins on different days of the week, but *Omnibus*, *Panorama*, *Churchill's People* and *Midweek* also came into this category. The remaining 45 series studied more or less followed the BBC1 'norm'.

For BBC2 programmes, the norm is for the audience amongst the 'As' to be about half as big again as amongst the 'Cs', but there were a number of occasions on which the differential was a good deal greater than this, notably for the serialisation of *Jane Eyre*, for *Second House*, for the serious music programmes on Sunday evenings, for *The Money Programme*, for Test cricket, and for *Pro-Celebrity Golf*. There were even a few BBC2 series to which the 'Cs' turned in larger proportions than did the 'As'. These were *Alias Smith and Jones* (transmitted at a time when both the other channels were carrying current affairs), *The Bachelors* and three series of films.

The socio-economic group profile of ITV audiences was the reverse of BBC2's, with 'C' group audiences normally being about twice as large as those amongst the 'As'. There was less variation in pattern than on the other channels, the nearest the 'A' group audiences came to closing the gap between them and the 'C' group audiences being for the play on Sundays at 10.15 p.m. and for the documentary series on Tuesdays and Fridays at 10.30 p.m.

As the examples quoted above indicate, the detailed results, series by series, suggest that a 'taste pattern' is superimposed on a 'channel pattern'. This is not easy to bring out clearly in numerical form, as grouping programmes into broad categories simply clouds the picture (*It Ain't Half Hot, Mum* and *Lulu* are both Light Entertainment, for example). What is more, the number of examples in some categories is small. However, expectations were borne out to the extent that differences between 'A' group and 'C' group audiences for most light entertainment and film series were found to be more tilted towards the 'Cs' than was the channel average, whichever channel they were on, whereas the reverse was true for most news, current affairs and documentaries.

2 Listening in the United Kingdom in 1975/6

Note

The estimation of the amount of listening is dependent to a much greater extent than is the estimation of the amount of viewing on the method used and on the 'operational' definition of listening that this method implies. After much consideration BBC Audience Research adopted, and has used ever since, a process of 'aided-recall' in which the samples of people interviewed are helped to remember what they were doing throughout the day 'yesterday', whether or not they were listening or viewing, and if so to which programme. This generally results in *smaller* estimates of listening than do some other methods commonly used throughout the world. The reasons why this should be so are not entirely clear but it seems highly likely that if two estimates disagree, the explanation is probably that 'it depends what you mean by listening'. Throughout what follows, the words 'as assessed by Audience Research's method' should be assumed to follow all estimates of listening.

After remaining steady for three years at an average of about $8\frac{3}{4}$ hours per head per week, listening to BBC Radio started to fall a little early in 1975. This was at least in part a result of the economy measures introduced at that time, which merged services for part of the day and shortened transmission hours. This fall has been confirmed by more recent results. Throughout the year under review the amount of BBC Radio 1 listening consistently fell short of that recorded a year earlier, though the difference was no more than some 40 minutes per head per week, a drop of about 7%. Nearly all the drop was in listening to Radios 1 and 2, the services most affected by the cuts and mergers, but also the ones most similar to the majority of ILR stations in content.

Until the beginning of 1976 the amount of listening to Independent Local Radio being recorded by the Department's continuous Survey could not be comprehensively estimated in the course of routine computer processing, though it was roughly estimated to be some 45 minutes per head per week. When regular quarterly estimates began to become available, from the first quarter of 1976, they proved to be somewhat greater than this – well over one hour per head per week. This more than compensates for the slight fall in BBC Radio listening and indicates that there has, in fact, been a modest upturn in the *total* amount of listening.

Despite the small decline in BBC Radio listening, it was, as usual, Radio 1 that attracted more listening than did any other channel (almost two-fifths of the total), Radio 2 coming next with more than one-quarter. Most of the rest was to the other BBC Radio services, with the commercial services, ILR and Radio Luxembourg, taking about one-eighth. Again as usual, some two-thirds of all listening was found to take place during the daytime between 9.00 a.m. and 5.00 p.m., and most of the rest before 9.00 a.m. It was only Radios 3 and 4 for which listening in the evenings made a substantial contribution – one-quarter of the total for Radio 3 and one-fifth for Radio 4.

In addition to providing estimates of the *amount* of listening, the continuous Survey yields statistics of the number of people who listen to anything at all on each of the radio services. These figures are commonly referred to as the 'daily patronages' of the services. On weekdays it is customary for patrons of radio to amount to about 45% of the entire population. Turning to the individual services, Radio 1's lead in the amount of listening – referred to in the preceding paragraph – is mirrored in the size of its daily patronage, almost 10 millions. Radio 2 follows with 8 millions, Radio 4 coming third with 6 million listeners on the average day. The next largest daily patronage figure is for Independent Local Radio, 2½ millions. In making comparisons between the figures for Local Radio and those for National Networks it is, of course, important to bear in mind that local services are not available in all parts of the United Kingdom. However, even if the comparison is restricted to those parts that *are* served by the ILR stations, the largest daily patronages recorded in 1975/6 were still those of Radios 1 and 2. Though the local estimates provided by the Department's Survey of Listening and Viewing are inevitably less reliable than are the national estimates, it appears that in only two or three of the nineteen ILR areas were the daily numbers of listeners to Radio 1 and Radio 2 rivalled or even overtaken by those of the ILR stations.

Most listeners listen to only one channel on a given day – about 40% of the 45% of daily patrons doing so. Nearly all the remainder hear programmes on two channels, and only about 1% listen to three or more channels. The few who *do* listen to more than one channel on 'the average weekday' in the main patronise Radios 1 and 2 or Radios 2 and 4. The service with the greatest exclusivity of usage is Independent Local Radio, very few of whose daily patrons (they amount to about 5% of the popula-

	Listeners on 'the average day' January/March 1976 to;							The population of the UK age 5 or over
	Radio 1	Radio 2	Radio 3	Radio 4	BBC Local Radio	Ind. Local Radio	Radio Luxembourg	
	%	%	%	%	%	%	%	%
Aged 5–14	14	9	—	2	1	4	13	16
15–29	43	17	18	12	12	38	71	23
30–49	28	34	33	29	33	36	13	27
50 or over	15	40	49	57	54	22	3	34
	100	100	100	100	100	100	100	100
Adults:								
Males in employment	39	35	46	29	34	47		35
Males not in employment (mainly retired)	6	12	17	18	11	6		14
All Males	45	47	63	47	45	53		49
Females in employment	25	16	11	13	17	36		17
Females not in employment (mainly housewives)	30	37	26	40	38	11		34
All Females	55	53	37	53	55	47		51
Socio-economic Group A	4	6	23	15	5	4	5	6
B	23	25	42	34	22	22	22	24
C	73	69	35	51	73	74	73	70
	100	100	100	100	100	100	100	100

tion) listen to BBC Radio at all on the same day. At the other extreme comes Radio 3, nearly half of whose daily patrons (about $1\frac{1}{2}\%$ of the population) also listen to another channel – generally Radio 4.

The kinds of people who make up the 'daily patronages' of the various radio services are compared in the table on page 17.

Some of the points which stand out in the table include:

(i) Patrons of Radio Luxembourg came overwhelmingly from the 15–29-year-old age group, Radio 1 and ILR also drawing above-average proportions of their patrons from this group – though to nothing like the same extent as did Radio Luxembourg.

(ii) Children of 5–14 years of age contributed significantly to the daily patronages of Radio 1 and Radio Luxembourg, and to a lesser extent of Radio 2, but *not* of ILR.

(iii) Radio 3, Radio 4 and BBC Local Radio found the bulk of their patrons in those aged 50 and over.

(iv) It is these age differences that underlie the rather narrower differences in terms of employment. There were comparatively high proportions of employed persons amongst the patrons of Radio 1, ILR and Radio Luxembourg, largely because fewer of them are housebound with children or are old enough to be retired.

(v) As far as socio-economic status is concerned, Radio 3 and Radio 4 stand out clearly from the other services. Not far short of one-quarter of the Radio 3 daily patrons were drawn from the small 'A' socio-economic group (mainly people in professional and higher managerial occupations, together with their families), as were one in seven of the Radio 4 patrons. It is in this group, of course, that appetite for such things as 'serious music' and 'current affairs' is most prevalent.

In conclusion, it must be emphasised that these figures relate to the patrons of a radio service on 'the average day'. Other published surveys have produced analyses of the kind of people who have listened in 'the average week' or 'the average month'. Though there will undoubtedly be similarities between the daily, weekly and monthly patronages, the correspondence cannot be expected to be exact.

3 Viewers' Reactions to some Television Programmes

Current Affairs

Nationwide, which follows the early evening News bulletin on BBC1 at 6.00 p.m., continued to attract an audience of about 7½ millions each weekday, most of whom were found to be well satisfied with the varied stories presented. There was a particularly warm response to the 1000th edition on Friday, 9 May. Though viewers thoroughly enjoyed the opportunity of looking back over the wide diversity of topics covered in 'the previous nine hundred and ninety-nine' programmes, the most interesting part of the broadcast, according to many, was the glimpse 'behind the scenes' at the amount of planning and hard work that goes into just one edition. It made them all the more appreciative of the 'back-room' workers as well as the very efficient studio team. Several added that they were 'already looking forward to the next thousand'.

An even longer-running ingredient of the BBC schedules is *Panorama*, now at 8.10 p.m. on Monday evenings. It is seen each week by about 4 millions. One of its best-received editions was its examination of Rhodesia ten years after UDI (10 November). Most of its viewers found it balanced and comprehensive, and thought that it had presented the conflicting viewpoints extremely well, even though there seemed to be no answer to the depressing fact that there was no easy way out or grounds for optimism. There was praise for the reporter, Richard Lindley, whose approach to the subject, viewers felt, had been both fair and searching, and who had obviously won the confidence of both sides.

There was a no more than moderate response to the first week of the new current affairs magazine *Tonight* (Monday–Friday, 1–5 September, at various times after 10.00 p.m.). Admittedly, only a few viewers found *nothing* to interest them in the programmes they saw, the main reason for the lukewarm reaction being the fairly widespread feeling that so far the series lacked an individual 'style' and was somehow less 'immediate' and topical than its predecessor at this time. Nevertheless, a substantial number found it varied, interesting and well presented (Sue Lawley being especially popular). Noteworthy amongst its early editions was its National

Health Week (27–31 October). Most appreciated being given some insight into the problems of what now 'really is a crisis', but also felt that 'there is no easy solution'. A minority, however, though held by the subject, found that the widely opposing viewpoints tended to confuse the issues rather than clarify them, and felt that some of those interviewed 'seemed more interested in forcing their personal opinions and prejudices' than having a rational discussion, thus leaving them 'as much in the dark as ever'.

Panorama and *Tonight* joined together on 17 November for 'The Devolution Debate', the *Tonight* part being a special 'phone-in'. Opinions differed markedly. For most, it seems that the 'general outline' given in the first part had been worthwhile and informative, the speakers (who included Edward Heath and Jeremy Thorpe) being commended for their calm and intelligent comments. These approving viewers also found their answers to callers' questions clear and informative, adding detail to the earlier material. However, a sizeable minority considered the coverage 'dull' and unilluminating, a fact that they attributed to the politicians' tendency to produce 'the same old arguments' which contained 'too many opinions and not enough facts'.

The Arts

The major artistic events of the year on BBC TV were the studio production of Wagner's *The Flying Dutchman* (9 November) and the Bolshoi Ballet performance of *Romeo and Juliet* (28 March). The Wagner opera was seen by about 600,000 viewers, most of whom were impressed by the imaginative staging and sets. The performance, too, with Norman Bailey memorable in the title-role, proved satisfying to most. However, a sizeable minority felt that the work had not adapted successfully to the small screen, and was not – in their view – the happiest choice of operas to televise.

Romeo and Juliet, too, though certainly enjoyable according to the majority of its 2 million viewers, was not, perhaps, quite as thrilling as some had hoped. There was warm praise for the dancing, scenery and choreography, and for many it was clearly an emotional experience to see one of the world's greatest companies performing in its proper setting. Others, however, felt that the pathos and simplicity of the Romeo and Juliet story was 'swamped' by spectacle and 'the sheer vastness of the Bolshoi stage' and, despite the 'wonderful achievement' of the television production staff, they were more than usually conscious of the limitations of the small screen.

The film commemorating the bicentenary of Turner's birth (22 April) was well received. Most viewers found the selection of his works suitably diverse and immensely enjoyable, their enjoyment being enhanced by what they felt to have been a high standard of narration and photography. The programme had increased their knowledge and understanding, they said. On the other hand, a sizeable minority had found the programme rather less stimulating than they had hoped, some attributing their disappointment to viewing in black and white which 'could scarcely do justice to Turner's paintings'.

Drama

The large and varied drama output cannot be adequately represented by any small selection, but the following notes at least reflect the diversity.

Though roughly half its viewers warmly welcomed the first of seven adaptations of stories by P. G. Wodehouse (23 April), the remainder had reservations concerning the humour in *The Truth About George*, turning, as it did, on the speech impediment of the main character, which they considered in doubtful taste. Others found it too slow-moving and out-of-date. Even so, there was high praise for both the acting and production.

Described on the one hand as 'disgusting' and on the other as 'poignant', David Agnew's play *Diane* (9 July) had a decidedly mixed reception. A number of viewers objected to the dreariness of the theme, the excessive use of bad language (a particularly sore point, this) and the fact that, through being badly cut – 'presumably for reasons of censorship' – the play was disjointed and difficult to follow. Others, however, evidently found the story unusual, interesting and moving, and were completely absorbed by it.

The fifth of thirteen episodes in the *Ben Hall* series on 3 August failed to make a very great impact, the majority of its viewers finding it slow-moving and lacking in action. The remainder, however, enjoyed the excitement, suspense and toughness of the characters, and there was overall approval for both acting and production.

Though *Angels* attracted far more viewers than did *Ben Hall* (8 millions against 3 millions), reactions have been equally mixed. For example, the episode on 22 September, a day in the Female Medical Ward, contained 'all the dullness of an average day', it was said, even the glimpses into the personal problems of some of the staff being unsatisfactory as 'nothing was followed through'. Others, however, welcomed the true-to-life atmosphere, unglamorous nurses who 'obviously work very hard', and the 'semi-documentary approach' which gave 'a good and pleasantly entertaining idea of what hospital life is like'.

The most noteworthy 'Play for Today' during the year was also concerned with hospitals. *Through the Night* (2 December) had, for most of its viewers, some pertinent and important things to say about the hospital/patient relationship, and made compelling viewing. There were those who found it disturbing – not to say distressing – but most felt that the 'taboo' subject of mastectomy had been dealt with both delicately and effectively, and there was warm praise for the realism of the play itself, for the acting, and for a production in which the 'stark, ugly, noisy and messy near-incompetence of a NHS public ward was uncannily brought to life'.

The controversial series of four films, *Days of Hope*, portraying the ten years leading up to the General Strike in 1926 through the lives of a politically inclined Yorkshire family, was generally praised for its moving realism, the writing 'conveying perfectly the conflicting moods of cynicism and idealism of the period'. Not all, of course, were so favourably impressed, some finding the theme drab, tedious and boring, whilst – though few dismissed it as 'distortion' – it was quite widely feared that the documentary format might lead some to accept as fact what was only one view (and, in some opinions, a biased view). Nevertheless, whilst regretting its 'rather disturbing left-wing bias', the majority gave warm praise to its 'realistic' acting and production.

The two-part adaptation of *Moll Flanders* (26 November and 3 December) was very well received, the adventures, amorous and otherwise, of Defoe's resilient and very likeable heroine making appealing entertainment, as well as giving a vivid insight into the harsh realities of a time when the lives of rich and poor were in marked contrast, viewers said. Although a minority found the second episode too 'compressed' or disappointingly slow after the spirited first part, there was widespread praise for an excellent performance and production.

The final episode of *Poldark* (18 January) marked the end of what had been, for most of its viewers, a thoroughly enjoyable serial. Set in a Cornish tin-mining community in the late eighteenth century, it was, they thought, a colourful, exciting and romantic tale, which gathered momentum as it went along. The sets, the costumes and the 'lovely Cornish scenery' were widely praised.

The Glittering Prizes, six plays about life at Cambridge and after, were enthusiastically received. However, while greatly impressed by the 'superbly perceptive' dialogue, some felt doubtful about the realism of the developing situations, many regarding them as quite untypical. A small minority also disapproved of too much swearing and 'a lot of undressing for the sake of it'.

The most enthusiastically received of the drama series was *When the Boat Comes In*, which was seen each week by about 13 million viewers, most of whom were delighted with it. They found it realistic and moving, and were impressed by what they regarded as a 'well-balanced mixture of tragedy and comedy'. There were a few criticisms – such as of a too-lavish family party – whilst others felt they would have enjoyed it more were it not for what they saw as a spate of industrial sagas of the 'cloth cap and cobblestone' type. Most, however, welcomed it unreservedly.

Light Entertainment

The new light entertainment series screened during the year proved a very mixed bag, in viewers' estimation. An interesting example of how a series can 'catch on' was provided by *The Good Life*, which started inauspiciously in April 1975, but finished its first short run with most of its viewers 'aching with laughter' and longing for its return. When it *did* return, in December/January, it was with a much increased, but equally delighted, audience. They described it as 'refreshing', 'true-to-life', 'hilarious', and were full of praise for the 'superb performances'.

The same could not be said of *Beneath the News*, which its viewers – almost without exception found laboured and pointless and, for many, in decidedly bad taste. Hopes that it might fill the need for a satirical series were dashed.

My Honourable Mrs was much less heavily criticised, but failed to live up to the expectations of its viewers, the best they could find to say about it being 'not terribly funny, but harmless'. Equally lukewarm was the response to *The Growing Pains of P.C. Penrose*, which struck the majority of its audience as slow and crude, with a weak storyline and laboured performances. There were, however, quite a few who derived considerable enjoyment from it and felt it had possibilities.

Reaction to *I Didn't Know You Cared* became decidedly more favourable as the series progressed and viewers 'got on to the authors' wavelength', though it never entirely lost the criticisms that its humour was silly, crude and distasteful. At the other extreme were those who enjoyed the blend of 'dry wit and broad humour', whilst most came somewhere in between, feeling that the series at best 'had some very funny moments'.

Though its audiences were much smaller than for *The Good Life*, *Fawlty Towers* was found equally hilarious. Played with pace and style, with 'characterisations to be treasured', this was 'visual comedy at its best', most of its viewers agreed.

Other Noteworthy Programmes

There was a largely unfavourable reaction to *Scenario: The Peace Game* (6 May). In the event, many viewers who had looked forward to the programme found that from a good beginning it soon became tedious and complicated, a situation which even James Burke's interjections failed to remedy. Many lost the thread and simply switched off. A minority, however, enjoyed the intellectual exercise, which enlarged their understanding of NATO and found that the inclusion among the 'players' of men with diplomatic, military or personal experience of these matters made it all seem very real.

Although not, perhaps, an outstanding programme, a 'slightly different' and quite revealing look at the public and private life of *Muhammed Ali* (5 August) was generally well received. Some viewers found the subject matter too familiar or its presentation confusing, but only a very few expressed real dislike of Ali himself, most being very favourably impressed by a man who, under the 'showmanship', struck them as honest, intelligent and sincere in his concern for the deprived members of his own race.

The 600th edition of *Top of the Pops* (9 October) attracted its usual large audience of about 11 millions, but was a little more coolly received than usual. Some of its viewers, for instance, thought that the occasion warranted a special programme (chart-toppers going back over the years, perhaps, as at Christmas time), others complaining that the format was dull and stale or the songs and artists this week rather poor. The majority, however, enjoyed it well enough.

Prince Charles, Pilot Royal (14 November) was thought to have provided an excellent insight into the life and training of the heir to the throne, but most interest naturally centred on the character and personality of Prince Charles. Almost without exception, viewers were greatly impressed by this 'very well-adjusted young man' possessing all the qualities one could wish for in a future king. Only a small minority, feeling that his natural reserve prevented them from seeing 'the real Prince Charles' or that the programme was 'thrown together' in rather arbitrary fashion, expressed even moderate disappointment.

Two major series of dramatised documentaries were *Churchill's People*, which ended its twenty-six-week run in June 1975, and *The Explorers* in September/November. The former had a decidedly lukewarm reception, though some episodes were much better than most, in viewers' opinions. For example, they felt that The Agreement of the People (21 April), which dealt with Cromwell's handling of a relatively little-known mutiny by extremists in the Parliamentarian army during the Civil War, had continued the general theme of the 'lower orders' ' fight for equality in a most interesting way. Although some were still disappointed by what they saw as another 'static' episode, in which the ratio of dialogue to action tended to make the time drag, the increasing realism of costumes, sets and general presentation was thought to have made the series more 'credible' and appealing. Even more favourable was the response to Mutiny (9 June). The course of the 1797 naval mutiny at Spithead and The Nore made a 'compelling' story, the 'sometimes horrific' realism creating a vivid picture of the 'unbelievable' hardships of the sailors' lives. In spite of some criticism of the 'bare' sets, the whole production was generally considered satisfactory, and the performances of a well-chosen cast very good.

The Explorers, on the other hand, was well received throughout. Typical of the reactions was that to the story of Burke and Wills (5 October) who crossed Australia from south to north in 1860/61. For the majority, the programme gave an impressively realistic account, with some insight into what viewers described as 'the human reasons for failure' of this ill-fated and badly planned expedition. Only a minority found the journey less impressive than most, the details confusingly complicated, and the suffering depicted hard to view. The pick of the bunch, however, was Cook's voyage to the South Pacific in 1770 (2 November), which intrigued its viewers with its picture of eighteenth-century seagoing life. They commended the 'restrained and lifelike' performances, and rhapsodised over the beautiful location filming.

It is very rare for *The World About Us* not to delight its viewers, but the edition on 30 November, African Masque, proved rather disappointing to most of them. A minority, it is true, found it interesting and instructive, agreeing that music and dance formed an integral part of African culture, but the majority felt that this artificial 'theatrical version' of traditional village dancing was out of place in a series predominantly concerned with wildlife and the natural features of the earth we live on.

For most of its viewers, *Spartakiada* from Prague (27 February) was 'a magnificent show', a unique display of harmony, health and vigour from Czech gymnasts massed at Europe's largest stadium, the Strahov. Though the majority warmed to the spectacle and were particularly impressed by the precision and timing of the performers, a minority found them somewhat chilling, occasionally observing that such 'accurately timed' athletics were tedious and boring. However, both Ian Wooldridge's commentary and the 'visually superb' presentation were widely praised.

4 Listeners' Reactions to some Radio Programmes

Radios 1 and 2

The DJ shows that occupy the great majority of the time on Radios 1 and 2, and which attract some three-quarters of all listening, were referred to at length in last year's Annual Review. This year, the emphasis is on other kinds of programmes.

Two contrasting record request programmes on Sundays were *The W1A 4WW Show*, presented by Anne Nightingale, and the long-running *Family Favourites*. The former had a somewhat mixed response. Whilst some listeners welcomed it enthusiastically as providing an interesting mixture of 'album tracks, oldies, and new singles' with 'not too much top 30 material', and had greatly enjoyed the style of presentation, others complained of 'too many heavy, obscure and boring' records and thought Anne Nightingale had a monotonous voice and not very lively manner for a show of 'all-round entertainment'. In between were those who, if regarding the programme as 'nothing really startling', found it all pleasant enough.

Most listeners to *Family Favourites* still seem to enjoy it as much as ever. Some commended the music as being tuneful and popular and felt that Sandi Jones and her colleagues overseas introduced the items in an agreeably 'personal' way. However, there were fairly widespread objections to the amount of talk – not so much the dedications as the 'mutual admiration society bit' between the various introducers.

A third record request programme, this time on Saturdays, is *Junior Choice*. Most of its listeners clearly approved the idea of devoting part of it to *Young Ideas in Action*, featuring children helping the less fortunate – on 21 February making toys for their disabled contemporaries. Besides finding the children's 'unaffected' talk on their project 'heartwarming', many hoped this would encourage others to think along these lines. There was some criticism from those either simply not interested or who found it rather hard to catch what was said, either because of the children's Northern accents or their 'tendency to mumble', but in the main they agreed the broadcast was most worthwhile, and a number wished it had been longer.

Listeners with problems of a different kind were the subject of *Contact* on 9 January, when Evelyn Home dealt with depression and bereavement. The range of reaction proved to be very wide. Half were of the opinion that it was a worthwhile programme, apparently believing – or at least hoping – that such a 'sympathetic' and knowledgeable approach might prove helpful to those in similar positions. However, amongst the others, reactions ranged from lack of interest – either because the problems were irrelevant to them or because such chats were just 'not their cup of tea' – to distinct impatience with the whole 'maudlin' programme. And even among those approving of the programme idea, there were a number who doubted the therapeutic value of so short a talk or of advising those affected 'to make an effort'.

Amongst the many music programmes to which reactions were obtained was *Melodies for You* on 20 July. This was a Sunday 'must' for many of its listeners who felt the series could always be relied on for attractive, mostly familiar and well-loved music, and who found this edition no exception. Though a minority thought him rather unctuous and 'sugary', David Jacobs was well liked by most, his quiet, pleasant voice, easy manner and 'odd anecdotes and reminiscences' adding interest to the music and 'making one feel "in" on a friendly get-together'.

Most listeners to *Ralph McTell* (20 April) found him 'a folk singer and songwriter of much appeal', it seems, though enthusiasts were disappointed that McTell had not introduced his own songs, and that the broadcast had not been in stereo. Quite a few, however, did not find him at all outstanding, whilst others simply did not care for this kind of music. Noel Edmonds' introductions were generally praised.

Most listeners to *Newsbeat* (Monday to Friday, 24–28 November) liked the lively way in which, 'briefly covering the essential news', it struck a good balance between serious and lighthearted items, including some on the pop world. Apart from a few who rather resented the intrusion of news on Radio 1, the main complaint among a dissatisfied minority was that the 'scrapbook' presentation, the jingles between items and the 'racy' tone, trivialised current affairs. On the whole, though, it appears that the 'modern', 'unstuffy' approach was considered well suited to Radio 1, making it for some at least something to be enjoyed instead of 'just another news programme'.

The light entertainment slot at 1.00 p.m. on Radio 2 included *The First of the Christmas Shows* (23 August), which received a very mixed response. The majority of its listeners were clearly irritated by its 'silliness', some being scornfully dismissive of it as 'one big yawn', while others found it rather offensive. However, its absurd brand of fun appealed to a sizeable minority, who found the 'slick, lively' sketches refreshing and praised the versatility of the team.

There was less adverse reaction to *Punch Line* (6 September) though the overall response was lukewarm. The game – in which three well-known personalities were asked to supply a 'punch line' for a number of comedy sketches – was welcomed as an excellent idea for a 'different' and potentially entertaining show, and was, in fact, enjoyed by a sizeable number of its listeners. Often, however, the ad-libs were considered pathetically unfunny and inadequate, so that for others the whole thing 'fell rather flat'.

For most of its listeners *The Family Brandon* (28 February) proved an amusing, lighthearted lunchtime interlude, with many well-timed gags and punch-lines, but it struck many others as predictable and unoriginal – 'merely a conglomeration of all previous situation comedies'. However, few found fault with the artists; Tony Brandon, in fact, often being likened to and compared favourably with Tony Hancock.

Nostalgia played a large part in the responses to two other shows. Listeners to the special edition of *In Town Tonight* (26 July), marking the move (after 32 years) of BBC Light Entertainment Department from Aeolian Hall to new premises near Broadcasting House, gave it a very warm reception. Only a few had reservations, either disliking the extracts from old editions, or because they thought this edition was not up to the standards of the old days.

I Remember George, a four-part series in October telling the story of George Formby, evoked happy memories of his wartime entertaining for most of its listeners, and revealed much they did not know about his personal background and method of working, through the reminiscences of those who knew him. To some listeners he was unknown or unfamiliar, but most found some interest in the career and in the 'still surprisingly enjoyable' singing of a 'great entertainer'.

The Saturday-afternoon sequence *Sport on Two* is invariably well received by its listeners – who usually number about three-quarters of a million. Some items inevitably appeal more than others, and some events prove to be much more exciting than others, but there is rarely anything but praise for the commentators – who succeed, it appears, in putting across the 'atmosphere' as well as the happenings – and for the well-varied selection of events.

Radio 3

One of the really outstanding events of the year, it was said, was the talk by *Solzhenitsyn* on 24 March, listeners repeatedly saying that they could not help but admit the truth of his criticisms of present-day Britain. There were those who felt that the greatest danger lay in the undue attention being paid to the 'vague rhetoric' of a man who, in their opinion, based his arguments on a vastly over-simplified view of the complex forces at work in British society, but the overwhelming impression was of a moving, thought-provoking and in every way outstanding broadcast by someone whose sincere concern lost nothing in the translation or reading – the latter being excellently done by Richard Pasco, it was said.

Almost as well received by the vast majority of its listeners was *A Song in the Night* (18 March), a monologue compiled from the letters and later poetry of John Clare. Most were moved by Clare's profound thoughts, simply and beautifully expressed, and whole-heartedly approved the presentation of this 'fascinating' study of insanity in an intellectual. It moved naturally towards a climax, they said, and there was warm praise for Freddie Jones (as John Clare), and for Roger Firth's skilful narration. A minority, however, would have preferred a documentary format, believing that more might have emerged about the poet's childhood and upbringing, which they felt must have had some bearing on both his creative abilities and his mental instabilities.

Also favourably regarded, though at a somewhat lower level of enthusiasm, was *New Dimensions of English Law* (12 October), the first of a series in which Lord Justice Scarman discussed aspects of English Law with lawyers and laymen. It was felt by most of its listeners to have been a valuable look at a subject 'which should interest us all'. They found the 'serious and intelligent' discussion between these 'dispassionate' speakers (Lord Justice Scarman, Lord Kilbrandon and Professor John Mitchell, chaired by Michael Zander) very stimulating, the logic with which the former argued the case for a Bill of Rights to protect individual liberties from infringement by Parliament impressing even those who remained unconvinced of the need for such a written guarantee. Only a minority found it all rather slow, dry and 'lacking in cut and thrust'.

Just as DJ shows are the main ingredient of Radios 1 and 2, so music is the main ingredient of Radio 3. Reactions to the music programmes, however, do little more than reflect opinion of the content – delight for Mozart, Beethoven, etc., and revulsion for much of the contemporary electronics. For example, *Music of the Masters* (4 October) was enthusiastically received by its listeners. Symphonies by Beethoven and Schubert and a Weber Overture, in the Swiss Radio recording of a concert given during the 1975 Zurich Festival, made ideal listening, they said, and gave a welcome opportunity to hear 'popular classics unspoilt by complex modern composers'. Only a small minority would have preferred a more varied choice of music and shorter introductions, or felt the conducting 'lacked sparkle'. Equally enthusiastic receptions were given to later programmes in the series.

Talks and features about music are generally more rewarding subjects for enquiry. This year's offerings included *My Dear Nimrod* (8 February), the story of the friendship between Edward Elgar and A. J. Jaeger, 'Nimrod' of the Enigma Variations, which was outstandingly well received. Its listeners felt that it gave a fascinating insight into the character and work of the composer at a 'crucial period' of his life, and most praised the 'sensitive' way in which the friends were 'allowed to speak for themselves'. The letters were thought to have been well read and interspersed with musical extracts of 'just the right length' to illustrate the story. Even so, a small minority found the presentation 'stodgy' and some would have liked more music or a 'slightly longer' programme.

Vocal Chords (23 February), on the other hand, clearly disappointed many of its listeners. There was, they thought, too much from the Radiophonic Workshop and not enough of the human voice (and that usually distorted) making a 'weird' mixture, a confused and disjointed programme, which appeared to have no unifying thread or logical progression and came over as a 'rag-bag' of sound that meant little, if anything. Those who did enjoy it, often did so less as a montage of sound than as an exercise in identifying the voices and/or occasions – 'not, I imagine, quite what the compiler intended'.

Another major element in the Radio 3 schedules is drama. *Iphigeneia in Aulis* (31 August) proved a most enjoyable production in which old and new forms blended very successfully. While a few found the dearth of 'action' and a lack of familiarity with the background made the thread difficult to follow, most – expressing particular regard for the classical dramatic approach to 'the great themes of life' – found it an absorbing and moving broadcast. The performance was generally praised, and those listeners who also heard Raymond Raikes' talk considered it a most helpful introduction which enhanced their appreciation of the play.

The rewriting by David Rudkin of *Hecuba* by Euripides (14 December) proved less successful. Whilst 'powerful and gripping' for a number of its listeners, who found it amazing that a work first staged in about the year 424 BC should still be so relevant, a number obviously found Greek tragedy heavy going, whilst others said the modern text and sound effects had jarred, the pace and style seeming uneven.

The Cookham Resurrection (11 May), a play based on Maurice Collis's biography of Stanley Spencer, aroused strong reactions. Most of its listeners welcomed it as an exceptionally vivid and successful evocation of the 'private world' that so much influenced Spencer's painting, but a substantial number found the kaleidoscopic impression of the artist's life, thoughts and work not only too far concerned with the 'most unsavoury' side of his character but so 'chaotic' in form as to be quite incomprehensible.

Saint Joan (2 November) enthralled the majority of its listeners, the powerful yet simple language and lively characterisations being said to be 'as fresh now as when it was first written'. Shaw's 'scarcely disguised' views were also relevant and thought-provoking in 1975, it was generally agreed. The opportunity to hear the Epilogue, often apparently for the first time, was welcomed by most, although a few considered it so 'wordy' and 'drawn out' as to be anticlimactic.

At the other extreme came *The Front Room Boys* (25 January) in the series New Australian Drama. This story of a year in an Australian office, month by month, was very coolly received. Described as 'totally witless', 'singularly pointless', even 'moronic', the writer had no idea, in the view of many, of how to convey boredom without boring. Some thought it an obvious and clumsy piece of Leftist propaganda, and others, while suspecting an underlying social message, said it had escaped them among so much 'dull', 'cliché-ridden' triviality. Only an extremely small minority enjoyed the play, the vast majority of its listeners switching off before the end.

Radio 4

The largest audiences for Radio 4 news and current affairs are for the morning sequence *Today*, usually heard by about 4 millions, followed by *The World at One*, 2 millions. The *evening* current affairs programmes, facing television competition, are heard by far fewer, but those who do listen in the main find them clear, informative and helpful. For example the *PM Reports* at 5.00 p.m. on 1 to 5 December were described by their listeners as a 'useful digest', even though some would have liked 'deeper coverage' and felt that the programmes sometimes sounded rather rushed. Listeners to *News Desk* (20 October) mostly thought its timing, format and presentation good, though a sizeable minority felt that there was too much news in general and that the programme was a reiteration of what had been heard earlier in the day. Although some found difficulty in concentrating fully after eleven o'clock at night, keeping abreast of the daily national and international economic events with *The Financial World Tonight* (28 July–1 August) proved stimulating to many of its listeners. It was 'easier than ploughing through the papers', they said, the clear, concise and reliable information presented by 'those who are directly involved', providing, for some, help in their business, and, for many who had no direct interest, an 'invaluable supplement to the news'. A minority, however, disliked the hurried delivery, or found difficulty in understanding the financial jargon.

The final programme of *In Our Time 1918–1939* (15 April) was among the most interesting of a fascinating series, listeners commented. Such 'recent history' broadcasts were welcomed both by those who had lived through the period and by younger listeners appreciative of more detailed information about times they had heard talked about or only dimly remembered. Illustrated so appropriately by archive recordings and satisfyingly presented, this had been 'radio at its best'.

Sex and the Young Person, in *Parents and Children* on 24 September, was thought by most of its listeners to be a very worthwhile subject. The majority felt that the points of view of parents and their children had been interesting and enlightening, whilst the 'experts' ' sensible and frank comments were welcomed. A minority, however, regretted that only a superficial study was possible in the time available, and that youngsters themselves would have been unable, because of the transmission time, to hear the broadcast. There was criticism, too, that there was no reference to 'Christian or any other kind of morality' and no mention of the medical dangers involved in sex before marriage.

Most listeners to *Workers' Co-operatives* (15 January) found its comparison between the profitable K.M.E. factory at Kirby and the failure of the *Scottish Daily Mail* interesting, and felt that the subsequent 'undogmatic' discussion between a panel of experts threw an informative light on the aims of co-operative enterprises, and on the conditions necessary for their success. A minority were only mildly appreciative, some dismissing it as 'dull' or saying they would have preferred more 'detailed' facts to the rather 'unwieldy' 'philosophical' discussion, but the majority found this a worthwhile appraisal of an important topic.

Checkpoint (28 November) is the 'shortest 25 minutes of the week' and, according to some, much too good to be 'stuck on Radio 4 in the morning when many of those interested, or likely to be, are out at work'. The series provided a most useful consumer service, it was thought, and this particular programme was well up to standard. The material was interesting and clearly presented, listeners said, and some important and sobering points were made, illustrating the not infrequent helplessness of the ordinary individual.

Radio 4's entertainment programmes proved a very mixed bag. There was a not very enthusiastic reception for the return of *Twenty Questions* (9 April), with a new chairman and three new panel-members joining its founder-member, Anona Winn. Many listeners felt it would take time for the newcomers to settle down, and most were optimistic, but a minority clearly thought this a change for the worse; or that it was too late to revive a programme that had gone on too long. In contrast, a sizeable group found it as entertaining as ever, some of them noticing a distinct improvement on last year.

Sandy Wilson's musical *Valmouth* (28 April) evidently gave very little pleasure, being described as 'shallow, trite, tasteless and witless, with grotesque characters, undistinguished music and banal lyrics and dialogue'. However, the main trouble appears to have been that listeners could often make neither head nor tail of it (indeed, many clearly gave up trying long before the end) and, despite what were undoubtedly good performances from, among others, Elizabeth Welch and Fenella Fielding, the overall feeling was that, however successful on the stage, as a radio production *Valmouth* had been little short of a disaster.

The Waltz King (24 October), on the other hand, a fictitious biography of Johann Strauss II, was very warmly received. Most of its audience found it very effective, and Elisabeth Bergner's voice and accent were so convincing that several thought the 'memoirs' were actually true. Strauss was said to have 'come alive' in her 'recollections' and the 'gaiety and joy' of old Vienna had been evoked, while there was praise, too, for the selection of Strauss's music, which charmed 'as always'.

Quote . . . Unquote (4 January), the first in a new quiz series about famous, and infamous, quotes from literature and history – with four panellists trying to guess their source – was no more than moderately appealing to most of its listeners. Some were particularly disappointed because, in their opinion, it was 'just another quiz', or 'vehicle for celebrities to show off their knowledge (or lack of it)'. However, a sizeable minority thoroughly enjoyed it and thought it a novel, 'super' new game which showed promise and that once it 'settled down' could well become a fast-moving, witty show.

'Get On With It', the last of four editions of *Kenneth Williams Playhouse* (22 July) had a very mixed response. Enthusiasts commended its 'varied and fast-moving revue-type format', which they regarded as an ideal vehicle for the 'versatile' Kenneth Williams. They were, however, counter-balanced by those preferring him in situation comedy and regarding the script as 'a ragbag of bits and pieces', the style of humour as unoriginal, sometimes too vulgar, or absolutely banal.

There was a warm welcome for the edition of *Week Ending* on 19 March, a series described by several of its listeners as one of the most witty and amusing on the radio. Some did feel that the programme was rather less funny and original than they would have expected – 'considering that the main news item of the week, the Prime Minister's resignation, must have been a gift to this team' – but they were very much in the minority and most had nothing but praise for both the script and the way it was put over by an excellent and versatile cast.

Reports on some ad hoc research studies

1 The Impact of the Radio and Television Coverage of the EEC Referendum Campaign

1 In order to monitor public opinion of the BBC's coverage of the EEC Referendum Campaign *during* the Campaign and to assess its impact after the Referendum had taken place, a three-pronged research project was undertaken as follows:

(i) An independent opinion research agency (ORC) was asked to add a few questions about the amount and unbiasedness of the coverage to routine national surveys* at intervals during the Campaign.

(ii) Audience Research interviewed a comparatively small 'panel' of people several times during the Campaign to discover what people regarded as the real issues of importance to them in coming to a decision, to tap their knowledge about the EEC and its institutions, and to relate these to their listening and viewing behaviour.
The sample of people selected for this 'panel study' was chosen at random from the Electoral Registers for 10 constituencies in the Birmingham conurbation. Its limitations were that it was neither particularly large nor was it strictly representative of the population of the United Kingdom as a whole. What is more, there was considerable attrition as the study progressed. 'First interviews' were successfully completed with 362 of the 520 originally selected, fourth interviews with 283, first and fourth with 249. (Most, but not all of them, also completed the second and third interviews.) Though they number less than half of the people originally selected, they do not show any substantial bias in such things as age, socio-economic group, political orientation, Trade Union membership and so on. Even so, they clearly cannot be assumed to be representative in other respects, particularly for example in terms of interest in the Referendum.

(iii) A national survey was made after the Referendum had taken place, to ask a wider range of questions about the coverage than could be included in

* Several market and opinion research agencies run regular weekly or fortnightly national surveys in which a wide range of questions are asked for many different clients. In ORC's Speedsearch surveys, the ones used in this project, nationwide quota samples of some 1000 persons are interviewed each week.

the national surveys *during* the Campaign, guided by the findings of the panel interviews. The sample for the post-Referendum survey consisted of 2400 names and addresses chosen at random from the Electoral Registers for 120 Polling Districts throughout the United Kingdom. The Polling Districts were selected with probability proportional to size of electorate. Successful interviews were made with just under 75% of those selected (or with a randomly chosen 'non-elector' when the named elector was found to be living elsewhere than at the listed address, or nearby).

2 The IBA agreed to participate in this research and to share the cost, and a Steering Group including Independent Television representatives was set up to oversee the project. The responsibility for the design and conduct of the work, however, remained with BBC Audience Research.

3 At the time the research plan was first devised, the date on which the Referendum would be held had not been settled, the most likely dates being believed to be either Monday, 23 or Thursday, 19 June. Even a date much later in the year, e.g. October, was regarded as a possibility. The fact that an earlier rather than a later date was likely had emerged when the Steering Group met on 25 March, so that it then seemed vital to start the questioning as soon as possible, in case the subject of the Referendum should – as seemed probable – begin to loom large in the newspapers and in broadcasting schedules in the next few weeks. Four questions to be added at intervals to their weekly Speedsearch surveys were quickly agreed with ORC, the first occasion on which they were asked being the week beginning 15 April and they were repeated at fortnightly intervals thereafter. This gave time for four 'waves', the final wave taking place in the week before Referendum Day (5 June). The first interviews with the Birmingham Panel sample were made between Friday, 18 and Sunday, 20 April. Two more 'pre-Referendum' waves followed at three-weekly intervals (i.e. on 9–11 May and 30 May–1 June) and a final wave *after* the Referendum, between 13–15 June. The national post-Referendum survey took place between 13–22 June.

Trends in Public Opinion During the Campaign

4 In the middle of April 1975, before the Campaign began, interest in the EEC and the forthcoming Referendum was restricted to a minority – even amongst the probably more-than-usually concerned Birmingham panel respondents. The first interviews with them showed that no more than 33%

felt that it would matter 'a lot' whether Britain remained in the Common Market or not, a further 26% believing that it would matter 'a little' and the same proportion that it would not matter at all. The remaining 15% did not venture an opinion. Only 31% said that being in the Common Market had made any difference to them personally. A bare majority (52%) felt that it was right to decide the issue of Britain's continued membership by Referendum, virtually all the rest feeling that Parliament should decide. This preference for devolving responsibility for deciding the issue onto their elected representatives in Parliament may well have owed something to the widespread ignorance of the public about the Common Market. More than half (54%) confessed to being 'very' or 'rather confused', and about the same proportion (51%) could not manage to answer correctly even one question of the six asked to tap their knowledge of the Common Market and its institutions. (For example, 'What are the other EEC countries?', 'Where does the European Parliament meet?', 'Can it take binding decisions?', etc.)

5 However, the Referendum had already become a topic of conversation, it seems, over 70% claiming that they had talked about the subject to family and/or friends, including 45% who said they had done so 'often'. In this it headed two other topics that were included in the questioning to provide a standard of comparison, repealing the Abortion Act (talked about by approximately one in four) and introducing a statutory Prices and Incomes policy (talked about by 64%). No more than 12% were undecided which way to vote, and most of those who had decided felt quite certain of their decision. At this early stage, both sides felt they were going to win, the 'intending-Yes' voters being a little more confident than were the 'No's'.

Belief in the Likely Outcome of the Referendum (mid-April)

	Those in favour of		
	staying in the EEC	*pulling out*	*Total*
	%	%	%
Think vote will go			
to stay in	67	26	53
to pull out	16	59	26
undecided	17	15	21
	100	100	100

6 The 'interested' – defined as those who said they were definitely going to vote and who thought it would matter a lot whether or not Britain remained in the Common Market – amounted to 30% of the sample, the uninterested being the larger number (45%) who either did not mind which way the vote went, or did not intend to vote, or did not think it mattered whether Britain remained in the EEC or not. The 'interested' were a little better-informed about the EEC (i.e. they were better able to answer the six questions about the EEC) than were the uninterested, though the difference was not great (average scores 0·85 and 0·62 respectively) – indeed, the surprise is that the difference was not greater. Many more of them than of the uninterested, however, were able to nominate a public figure whom they felt had been representing *their* point of view (55% against 27%). But for both groups, the person most frequently nominated was Edward Heath.

7 Three weeks later (early May), when the second interviews with the panel took place, not much change appeared to have occurred. Admittedly, the Campaign could hardly have been said to have started by then. No one in the sample had been 'canvassed', the promised pamphlets (from the Government, the pro-Europe organisation 'Britain in Europe' and the anti-Europe organisation 'The National Referendum Campaign') had not yet been distributed and very few people had attended a public meeting – in part, they claimed, because there had not been any they could have attended. There had, however, been frequent mention of the Referendum in broadcast news bulletins and in the newspapers. Compared with the position at the first interview, slightly *fewer* felt that a Referendum was the right way to decide the issue, just as many felt confused about the issue, whilst the proportion who had talked about the EEC with family and friends was distinctly smaller.

8 The answers to a different set of 'knowledge questions' did not suggest much general improvement. 44% knew – or more likely guessed right – that the EEC population exceeds that of the USA, and 30% correctly named Giscard d'Estaing as President of France. But hardly anyone knew how many European Commissioners there were, or how they were chosen, and only one person in five could name one or both of the British Commissioners – who had appeared on the television screen in many news bulletins at the time. This applied both to those who at the first interview had been classed as 'interested' and to those classed as 'uninterested'. Neither of these groups was any more likely at this stage than they had

been in mid-April to name a public spokesman who had put their point of view (54% of the former and 28% of the latter did so), and of those who did, it was still Edward Heath who led the field. The proportions supporting the 'stay in the EEC' and the 'pull out' positions were much the same (62% and 18% respectively) and about one-seventh remained undecided about which way they were going to vote.

9 However, the apparent stability was to some extent illusory, hiding changes of position on most of these topics in both directions. Thus it was not only 3% who had changed their decision about which way to vote – as might have been inferred from a cursory examination of the overall results – but 23%! Admittedly, few had actually *reversed* their decision (only 4%), most of the 'changers' being people who had made up their minds after being undecided at the first interview, or rather more frequently, who had become undecided! Similarly, it was not 6% who had changed camp on the question of whether or not a Referendum was the right way to have the issue of continued EEC membership decided but 19%. These were the ones who actually changed from one side to the other, a small number more either making up their minds or becoming undecided. The fluidity of opinion is evidenced most vividly by the changes in the subjective feelings of clarity about the issues. Only two-thirds remained clear or remained confused – and even a sizeable minority of those 'non-changers' in fact changed in the *degree* of clarity or confusion they laid claim to (e.g. from 'reasonably' to 'completely' clear, from 'rather' to 'very' confused, and so on). As many as 13% who three weeks earlier had felt themselves clear now felt confused, and 15% moved in the opposite direction.

10 Answers to the questions about repealing the Abortion Act and about introducing a Statutory Prices and Incomes Policy, which were also asked again in the second interview, provide a standard of comparison. The extent to which opinion changed on both of these issues in fact *exceeded* that observed in respect of the EEC Referendum. For a quarter to a third of the population to change their minds on important issues in a period of only three weeks is by no means unusual, it seems.

11 The third interviews took place at the end of May, on the Friday to Sunday preceding Referendum Day. The proportion who were undecided which way to vote had by then halved (from 12% in the first interview to 6%), and an even higher proportion expressed their intention to use their vote

(93% compared with 87% in earlier interviews). By this time, 26% had changed from their first interview position on the voting intention question – 8% reversing their original intention, 12% having made up their minds and 6% having become undecided. On balance, the intending Yes voters had increased from 62% to 68%, the intending No voters increasing only from 21% to 22%.

12 An awareness that the decision was likely to go in favour of staying in the EEC had by this time become widespread, 72% believing this to be the likely outcome, compared with 52% in the initial interviews. Even the intending No voters had, by this time, in the main realised that they were probably backing a loser.

Belief in the Likely Outcome – First and Third Panel Interviews

	1st Interview Intend to vote		*3rd Interview Intend to vote*	
	Yes	*No*	*Yes*	*No*
	%	%	%	%
Believe vote will go in favour of				
staying in the EEC	62	45	81	51
pulling out	18	38	6	29
undecided	20	17	13	20
	100	100	100	100

Once again, the movement was not all one way. One in five of those who originally thought the vote would go in favour of staying in the EEC did *not*, at this late stage in the Campaign, any longer think so – they were either of the opinion that it would go the other way or were undecided, in equal numbers. One in five of those who originally thought the No's would win continued in this belief, but two-thirds of them had swung over to the opposite point of view – the rest of them were 'don't knows'.

13 In the three weeks since the second interviews, the Campaign had really got under way, the media coverage had been extensive and all the publicity had been going full blast. Many more people claimed to have seen and heard programmes about the Referendum (other than news bulletins), 73% saying they had recently seen television programmes on the subject, for example, compared with 23% at the beginning of the Campaign. The proportion who had recently read newspaper articles about the Referendum, however, was – at 65% – no greater than in the first interviews.

Another important element in the Campaign was the distribution of the three pamphlets to virtually every household in the country. At the third interview, 56% said they had read all or part of them and most of the rest expressed their intention of doing so. On the other hand, there had been very little door-to-door canvassing – at least in the Birmingham conurbation where these panel interviews were conducted – and only a few people (2%) had attended a public meeting on the subject. More of those who at this stage intended to vote Yes than of those intending to vote No 'involved' themselves in the Campaign by watching or listening to programmes about the Referendum and by reading about it.

14 Despite all these Campaign activities, the extent to which the topic was talked about was no greater than at the initial interviews. Knowledge of the EEC remained at a rather low level. 37% knew or guessed correctly that 'the economic resources of the EEC exceed those of the US', but hardly anyone knew the name of the Prime Minister of Italy or that Mr Callaghan represented Britain on the Council of Ministers of the EEC. There was one area, however, in which considerable change *was* recorded, viz. in the public figures nominated by people as having expressed views that they themselves held. Edward Heath was overtaken as the most frequently nominated individual by Roy Jenkins – previously rarely nominated – whilst Wedgwood Benn came into third place close behind Heath. In addition to these changes, the appearance of many other well-known figures in radio and television programmes greatly widened the *range* of nominations.

15 The fourth and final interviews were made some ten days after Referendum Day. Not quite all of those who said they would vote in fact did so, nor did all vote as they originally intended to.

Changes between Intention at First Interview and Actual Vote*

	Voting intention in 1st Interview		
	Stay in	*Pull out*	*Undecided*
	%	%	%
Voted Yes	84	13	64
No	9	67	27
Didn't vote	6	19	6
Wouldn't say	1	1	3
	100	100	100

* The actual votes cast were in the ratio 67:33.

In fact, the proportion who voted as they intended to in the initial interviews was 68%, 8% voting the opposite way and another 8% not voting at all. A further 16% who were undecided at first, in the event *did* use their votes. However, on balance, the proportions voting Yes and No were very much in line with the originally stated intentions, with 64% voting Yes and 22% No as against 62% and 21% in mid-April.

16 Though such a high proportion of this panel sample voted in the Referendum, a majority still believed that it should not have taken place. Only 41% were of the opinion that a Referendum was the right way of deciding the issue, the same proportion as in the third interviews, but a considerably smaller proportion than held this point of view in the first interviews (52%). Two-thirds stuck to their views on this point throughout the Campaign, nearly all the rest (25%) changing sides.

17 By the end of the Campaign, most (75%) had read all or part of the three pamphlets (which virtually everybody said they had received by the time of the *third* interviews) and there had been a lot of coverage in the media – too much, according to a very sizeable minority – but still virtually no canvassing. Not surprisingly, in view of all the coverage, the number admitting to being confused about the issue fell, from 50% in the first two interviews to 24% in the fourth. This was accompanied, however, by no more than a modest improvement in the ability to give correct answers to the questions about the EEC – the same questions as were asked in the first interviews eight weeks earlier. (The answers were not, of course, given then.) Over a third still failed to score even one mark, and only one-sixth correctly answered three or more questions out of the six asked. Finally, perhaps because memory of the broadcast coverage had faded somewhat, there were further changes in the nominations people made of 'spokesmen putting their points of view'. Edward Heath regained his position as by far the most frequently nominated person, as he had been throughout most of the Campaign, with Roy Jenkins taking second place.

Public Opinion of the Broadcasting Coverage

Amount of Coverage

18 The first of four questions asked in the ORC surveys during the Campaign concerned the amount of coverage on radio and television. As the figures in the table facing show, almost half of those prepared to give an opinion were content with the amount, and there was little criticism on the score of

excessive coverage on any of the television and radio channels, at least until the end of May. Rather the reverse, in fact, very substantial minorities feeling that there was *insufficient* coverage. However, in the week before the Referendum (26 May–1 June), opinion shifted noticeably, with more than a quarter feeling that too much coverage was being given on television and only half this number taking the opposing point of view. At the same time, the proportions for whom the coverage was 'about right' increased slightly. Such dissatisfaction as there was of the amount of coverage did not, it seems, imply that there had been too much about the

Public Opinion About the Amount of Television Coverage of the Referendum Campaign

		Wave			
		1 *15–20 April* %	*2* *29 April– 4 May* %	*3* *13–18 May* %	*4* *26 May– 1 June* %
Amount of Coverage of Referendum on					
BBC TV	Far too much	7	7	7	12
	A bit too much	7	9	7	15
	About right	34	33	38	45
	Not enough	30	31	29	15
	Don't view/undecided	22	20	19	13
		100	100	100	100
ITV	Far too much	6	5	6	10
	A bit too much	7	9	6	12
	About right	30	30	32	37
	Not enough	30	30	31	14
	Don't view/undecided	27	25	25	27
		100	100	100	100

Referendum altogether, but simply 'too much too late'. (It should be noted in this context that if it had not been for a strike that kept ITV off the screen for a week, the number of programmes about the Referendum just before the last wave of interviewing took place would have been greater still. The major ITV Referendum programmes were rescheduled for the few days immediately before the Referendum, but this was after the end of the final wave of ORC interviewing.) Opinions about the amount of *radio* coverage followed much the same pattern as did those about television, once allowance is made for the substantial proportions who did not answer on the grounds that they listened too little to be able to judge.

19 People were asked to categorise themselves as being completely clear, moderately clear, rather confused or very confused about the issues involved in the EEC debate. They split fairly evenly between the clear and the confused, with about one-tenth 'completely clear' and the same proportion 'very confused'. This was so in all four waves, the proportion feeling confused showing no more than a very small decrease as the Campaign progressed. However, not many of those admitting to being confused showed much confidence in the possibility that the broadcasting coverage might reduce their confusion. Admittedly somewhat higher proportions of the confused than of those who claimed to be clear about the issues felt that there was not enough about the Referendum. But by the fourth wave, not many of them (only 18%) continued to feel that the coverage was insufficient, fewer than took the line that it was excessive.

20 The post-Referendum survey confirmed that the trend towards the position that the coverage had been excessive had continued, about one person in every four interviewed in the week after the Referendum expressing the view that BBC TV's and ITV's coverage had been 'far too much' and almost as many more that it had been 'a bit too much'. At the same time, the proportion feeling that it had not been extensive enough fell from 15% to 6%. Presumably people had forgotten the slow start to the Campaign coverage and were reacting to what they saw as a too-heavy concentration of peak-hour programmes in the last few days. Alternatively, they may have been expressing a general attitude derived from past experience and a sense of relief that the affair was over, without really considering the actual amount of coverage. Or it may have been a natural reaction to the fact that, after the Referendum, the material seen and heard no longer had any direct utility.

21 The late swing in opinion towards the 'too much' position was so substantial that criticism on this score approached the high levels recorded in respect of the two General Election Campaigns in 1974. The General Election surveys were made, as was the post-Referendum survey, a week or two after Polling Day, and hence the comments made about the basis of the replies in the preceding paragraph apply to them also.

22 Those who felt the television coverage to have been excessive were of many different kinds. Indeed it is striking that *all* sub-groups studied – men and women, the different age groups, people with different educational backgrounds, etc. – replied to this question in very much the same way. A

study of many other factors that might have been related to opinion on this point also proved abortive, the only one showing even a slight relationship to views on the amount of coverage being 'how long ago the decision to vote Yes or No was taken'. A little over half said that they had decided long before the Campaign started which way they would vote, two-fifths that it was more recently than that (including one in fifteen who were undecided right up to the day itself). Those who had decided long ago were slightly more inclined to complain of excessive coverage than were the others but even this relationship was very weak.

The Unbiasedness of the Coverage

23 The other issue on which public opinion was sought during the Campaign concerned perceptions of the unbiasedness of the coverage. As the figures below show, there was comparatively little criticism on this score and, moreover, what little there was early in the Campaign had almost disappeared by the end. This applies to both television services, to BBC national radio and to both BBC and independent local radio. Most people were also satisfied with the unbiasedness of the Press, despite the fact that all of the main dailies advocated voting Yes! In studies of the General Election Campaigns, newspapers have generally been felt to be *less* impartial than broadcasting.*

24 Those intending to vote 'No' in the Referendum, i.e. favouring pulling

Dissatisfaction with Unbiasedness of Coverage by Those Intending to Vote 'Yes' and 'No'

	Proportions dissatisfied with impartiality of coverage on									
	BBC TV		*ITV*		*BBC national radio*		*BBC local radio*		*ILR*	
	Intend to vote Yes %	*Intend to vote No* %	*Intend to vote Yes* %	*Intend to vote No* %	*Intend to vote Yes* %	*Intend to vote No* %	*Intend to vote Yes* %	*Intend to vote No* %	*Intend to vote Yes* %	*Intend to vote No* %
Wave										
1	12	20	12	15	5	8	3	5	3	3
2	10	21	10	18	5	9	2	6	2	5
3	6	13	6	11	3	4	2	2	2	2
4	2	12	3	6	1	3	1	1	–	1

* Statements of opinion such as these may, of course, derive more from preconceptions or from stereotypes of the media than from perceptions of actual examples of bias. 'Follow-up questions' to explore the origins or bases of the replies were beyond the scope of this particular operation.

THE POLYTECHNIC

out of the EEC, included a larger critical minority than did those intending to vote 'Yes', but both groups showed reductions in the level of criticism as the Campaign drew to its end. The intending 'No' voters were rather more critical of BBC TV than of ITV and, though the criticism of both channels fell off by about the same amount, 12% of the 'No' voters in wave 4 remained dissatisfied with BBC TV, as compared with 2% of the 'Yes' voters. The corresponding figures in respect of ITV were 6% and 3%. More pro-'Yes' than pro-'No' bias was discerned, it seems, even by those who intended to vote Yes; in contrast to recent studies of General Election Campaigns in which most of the alleged bias has been seen as being in favour of parties other than the one actually voted for. The balance of opinion about the direction of the bias was, however, far more even amongst the intending 'yes' voters than amongst the intending 'no' voters.

25 A somewhat different question asked in the post-Referendum survey revealed equally small numbers of severe critics of the media. About half felt BBC TV coverage to have been reliable 'all or most of the time', and only a few, one in fourteen, that it had rarely or never been trustworthy. ITV's coverage was judged slightly less favourably, though the proportion of severe critics was equally small. BBC Radio came out best of all, with two-thirds of those expressing an opinion saying that they had found the coverage reliable at least most of the time. Replies to a similar question about 'the reports and articles in the morning newspaper you yourself read' and in 'newspapers in general' showed that people rated 'their own paper' very much the same as they did the television channels but were considerably more critical of papers in general.

26 There were no significant differences between the replies of Labour, Conservative and Liberal supporters, or between Trade Union members and non-TU members. Even the 'Yes' voters and the 'No' voters did not differ greatly in this respect. The 'No's' contained rather bigger critical minorities – for example 11% of No's as against 4% of Yes's considered BBC TV's coverage 'rarely or never' reliable, but even so, slightly more of them (13%) voted it 'always' reliable. However, the differences, though not large, were big enough to swing the balance of opinion over from the 'Yes's' position in which a substantial majority voted the coverage 'always' or 'mostly' reliable to one in which a majority of the 'No's' adjudged it 'sometimes' or 'rarely' reliable. Whether the coverage *did* leave something to be desired in its presentation of the 'No' side of the argument or

whether the 'No's' tended, in defeat, to take a somewhat jaundiced view cannot be decided on this evidence alone.

27 All in all, it is as if the debate had been full enough for virtually everyone to feel that all views had been given a reasonable airing. (If this were so of the Press as well as of broadcasting, it would account for the exoneration of the Press on the issue of bias despite the pro-Europe editorial stands.) There may have been concern over the amount of coverage but perhaps it was this very prodigality that offered the means by which widely differing views could be seen to have been expressed.

The Contribution Made by Broadcasting

28 Answers to a question in the post-Referendum survey revealed that most people felt that 'broadcasting had helped them' (at least a little) in a number of respects. Of the five ways enquired about in which the broadcast coverage of the Campaign might have been found helpful, the ones most frequently endorsed by viewers and listeners were the 'peripheral' ones – 'showing what sort of people the leading campaigners were', and suggesting 'how the vote would be likely to go'. Then came the ones concerned with the conveying of information, viz. explaining what the main arguments of the pro and anti organisations were and 'telling you about the EEC and how it is run'. 'Helping to decide which way to vote' came last, more than half denying that broadcasting had helped at all in this respect. Though the replies given to a question such as this can only be subjective assessments of the usefulness of the Campaign, there seems little reason to doubt the validity of the broad conclusion that broadcasting contributed most significantly in filling in the background, and was less useful in conveying hard information or in changing attitudes. (This has been a finding in several earlier pieces of research throughout the world.)

29 The detailed research design made it possible to go some way beyond these subjective statements about the 'helpfulness' of the Campaign and to examine some of the ways in which broadcasting might have contributed more objectively, taking into account other possible contributory factors at the same time. This was done for five of the possible contributions that broadcasting might have made, viz.

(i) stimulating interest in the Referendum,
(ii) changing the subjective feeling of clarity or confusion about the issues,
(iii) increasing knowledge of the EEC and its institutions,

(iv) influencing what people thought of as the deciding factors when making up their minds which way to vote,

(v) contributing towards people's decision to vote rather than not vote, and which way to vote.

Interest in the Referendum

30 The ORC surveys during the Campaign revealed little change in the proportion of the population who claimed to be interested in the EEC Referendum. The panel interviews in the Birmingham area could not yield directly parallel data as no direct 'degree of interest' questions were asked. Instead, 'initial interest' was inferred (see para. 6) from the answers to several of the questions asked in the first interviews. 'Final interest' was similarly inferred, the group categorised as 'interested' at the end of the Campaign being defined as those (a) who had voted, (b) had made a special point of viewing at least a few Referendum programmes, and (c) had read the three pamphlets that were distributed to every household in the country. 25% fell into this category, i.e. 5% fewer than were classed as 'interested' in the first interviews. At the other extreme were those who, just before the Referendum, said they did not mind whether Britain stayed in the Common Market or not, and/or 'switched off Referendum programmes', and/or did not read the pamphlets. This accounted for 46%, the same number as were put into this category at the outset.

31 Those who were interested at first did not all fall into the 'interested' category at the end, nor did all those uninterested at first remain in that category. Very far from it. As many as 41% of the initially interested group had moved into the uninterested group by the end of the Campaign and 23% of the uninterested were classified in the final interview as interested. The static national picture revealed by the surveys during the Campaign thus appears to have arisen because of very substantial 'cancelling out' movements in both directions.

Changes in Interest in Campaign

		1st Interview	
	Interested	*Lukewarm*	*Uninterested*
	%	%	%
4th Interview			
interested	29	21	23
lukewarm	29	38	26
uninterested	41	41	52
	100	100	100

32 Detailed study of the replies suggests that some of those who constituted the initially-interested group did not in any absolute sense become less interested in, or concerned about, the question of Britain's membership of the Common Market. Rather, they seem to have become bored by a Campaign that was, for them, supererogatory. They had made up their minds which side to support (81% were quite certain as early as the first interview), they fully intended to vote, they felt reasonably confident of their judgments, most were not subject to conflicting views in their homes or from their friends, so what was there to Campaign about? On the other hand, some of those who were initially uninterested, who had not then made up their minds (40% of them had not), who knew little about the issues, who were confused, and who did not enjoy a 'congruent environment' became caught up in the debate. Almost certainly broadcasting and the Press played a considerable part in this, the use made of the media coverage by those who became interested during the Campaign being considerably greater than was that of the rest of the sample.

Change in Interest and Use of Media Coverage

	Change in interest between 1st and 4th interviews		
	Became interested %	*Remained same* %	*Became less interested* %
Use of media coverage			
below average	9	25	25
average	40	32	36
above average	43	36	30
Unclassifiable	8	7	9
	100	100	100

33 Those who became interested were also much more likely to have talked about the Referendum with their family and friends, towards the *end* of the Campaign but not at the beginning. What is more, it was not only their interest that changed. Those whose interest increased started by being slightly *less* able to answer the knowledge questions, but finished *better* able to do so. They started feeling more confused, and finished feeling less confused.

Feelings of Clarity about the Issues

34 As has been seen (para. 17), people's subjective feelings of clarity or confusion changed considerably as the Campaign progressed, the 'clear'

increasing from 43% to 72% with a corresponding decrease in the 'confused'. The *final* position left 24% of the Birmingham panel sample still confused – not very different from the national estimate provided by the post-Referendum survey, 30%. Though these feelings of clarity or confusion were only subjective assessments, they were consonant with the replies given to many other questions. The 'completely clear' were nearly all (88%) certain in which way they were going to vote at the very first interview, compared with only 37% of the 'very confused'. 73% of these very confused people said, nevertheless, that they intended to vote; but even more (94%) of the completely clear did so. Those who felt clear were decidedly better informed – or not quite so badly informed – about the EEC. 71% of them believed that the vote would go in favour of staying in the EEC, only 50% of the very confused feeling that this would be the outcome. Differences such as these between the clear and the confused continued to the end.

35 Comparing first and fourth interviews, 31% of the panel sample consisted of people who were initially confused but became clearer later. A few (4%) started clear and became confused, many others (24%) varying in the degree of clarity or confusion they expressed. The feelings of the remainder (about 40%) did not change, even in degree. These 'non-changers' proved to be people of all kinds and, in particular, nothing like all of them were 'clear' at the beginning of the Campaign. In this small panel sample – as in the much larger post-Referendum survey – those who remained unclear to the end used the broadcast coverage *less* than did those who were by then clear. (A good deal less, in fact, whereas in the post-Referendum survey the difference between the clear and the confused in this respect was not great.) The panel interviews also showed that those who started unclear avoided, or did not seek out, the broadcasting and press coverage right from the start, and that comparatively few of them talked about the subject to family or friends.

36 Most of those who felt unclear at the beginning of the Campaign and became clear, or less unclear, as it progressed, used the media coverage as much as did those who did *not* change in their feelings of clarity, i.e. from being part of a group of below-average media users, they became average (though not above-average) users. They also talked about the Referendum as much, having at first been less likely to do so. Even so, it is noteworthy that quite a few – one in five – of those who felt that they had become clearer did so *without* making much use of the media coverage. Un-

expectedly, the few people who became less clear, or more unclear, included a high proportion of above-average media users. If they were seeking enlightenment, they apparently did not feel they had found it.

37 If the figures are looked at 'the other way round', it emerges that above-average users of the media coverage were no more likely to 'become clear' than were below-average users (about 40% in each case). Much the same proportion in both groups did not experience any change in their feelings. These non-changers, however, seem to have been of two kinds: (a) those who remained unclear throughout, most of whom did not make much use of the media coverage, and (b) the larger number who remained clear, most of whom did. The contribution of the coverage was mainly to help those who were clear to stay that way, it seems, not to clear up the confusion of the others.

The Conveying of Information

38 The extent to which people were well-informed about the EEC was explored briefly in the first interview with the Birmingham panel and in the post-Referendum survey by asking six questions that were meant to range from relatively easy (e.g. to name the other countries in the EEC) to very difficult (e.g. how the members of the European Parliament are chosen). In fact, *all* were difficult, it seems, and the resultant 'knowledge scores' low. One person in three in the post-Referendum survey could not correctly name as many as four of the other eight Common Market countries and only one in five correctly named seven or eight of them. A larger minority believed Willy Brandt still to be the Chancellor of Germany than nominated Schmidt (only 10% did so). No more than a handful (4%) knew that the European Parliament meets in Strasbourg – 53% said Brussels! Fewer still knew that it is only the Council of Ministers that can take binding decisions or that Britain's representatives at the EEC Parliament are nominated by the political parties. The amount of Referendum coverage seen on television had no direct bearing on the ability to answer these questions correctly, though hearing several programmes a day on the radio apparently did make a little difference.

39 Before concluding that radio programmes contributed significantly to people's knowledge of the EEC, however, it was necessary to check that some other factor was not at work that affected both listening and knowledgeability. Educational background was an obvious candidate. A

thorough examination,* studying a large number of possibly influential factors all at once, led to the clear conclusion that it was educational background and sex (men being much better informed than women) that did by far the most to determine level of information, followed by 'age' (the elderly being better informed than the young) and only then 'the frequency with which radio programmes about the Referendum were heard'.

40 More detailed information was available from the Birmingham panel sample. Their average 'knowledge score' when they were first interviewed in April was 0·70 (out of 6), i.e. not far short of the average score of the national sample in the post-Referendum survey in mid-June. By this time the panel sample (asked the same questions once again) had increased their average score to 1·20. Clearly, they were either better informed to start with, or they had been conditioned by being reinterviewed periodically into being more receptive of information about the Common Market, or more probably, both. However, even amongst this relatively strongly motivated group, the magnitude of the improvement in score was not great. This is not surprising, perhaps, in view of the fact that the basic television and radio coverage, i.e. the news and current affairs programmes with the largest audiences, tended to be concerned more with reporting the arguments about the issues than with conveying information about the EEC.

41 It has sometimes been suggested that the mass media increase, rather than decrease, the current affairs 'knowledge gap' between the well informed and the ill informed, the former getting more out of the media coverage either because they watch, listen or read more, or because the material assumes too much background knowledge and hence leaves the ill informed behind. The converse seems to have occurred in the Referendum Campaign. It was not those who scored most in the first interview who made the greatest improvement, but those who scored least. Half of the 'nil scorers' at the first interview managed to do better the second time (they could not do worse), as did half of those who scored 1; though a further quarter of these fell back to zero. Similarly large minorities of those scoring 2, 3 or more also did less well in the fourth interview – and there was, of course, more opportunity for them to do so more drastically. These decreases in score largely cancelled out the gains made by others.

* For this purpose the technique known as 'multiple classification analysis' was used. It finds the best way of 'predicting' the knowledge score by allotting weights to the different factors included in the analysis. Educational background received the greatest weight, sex the next, and so on.

42 An indication of the extent to which such improvement in knowledge about the EEC as there was can be credited to the media coverage is given by the following table.

Changes in Knowledge-Score by Amount of Use of Media

	Use of Media Coverage		
	Above average %	*Average* %	*Below average* %
Fourth interview score *lower* than 1st interview score	14	8	15
Fourth interview score *same* as 1st interview score	26	41	50
4th interview score *greater* than 1st interview score	60	51	35
	100	100	100

Half of those who said they saw, heard or read little about the Referendum during the Campaign (the below-average media users) picked up no more information as the Campaign progressed, 15% doing less well the second time and the remaining 35% doing better. Of the above-average media users, on the other hand, though a similar proportion (14%) scored *less*, almost twice as large a proportion (60%) *improved* their score.

43 The fact that more above-average media users than below-average media users scored more the second time around does not conclusively *prove* that the above-average users picked up their new knowledge from the media. In an attempt to settle the issue, the data were subjected to 'causal path analysis', a procedure that sorts out – and weighs up – the contribution of variables that may lead to a particular outcome, in this case 'increase in knowledge score'. Unfortunately, the correlations between the variables were all so low that no significant result was obtained. (This was partly due to the comparatively small numbers of cases involved.) Despite this, the weight of evidence seems to point fairly definitely to a contribution, albeit a modest one, made by the media coverage to the public stock of information about the EEC.

The Decisive Issues

44 People's perceptions of the issues, as far as they themselves were concerned, were explored by asking them to say in their own words 'what the real, deciding factors were when you made up your mind which way to vote'.

Inevitably, many people were rather inarticulate or at best very unspecific, and this presented considerable problems in the coding or classifying of the replies. After several attempts had been made that proved to be either abortive or unilluminating, a workable solution was devised that attempts to group the factors into four categories and, within the categories, into those that could reasonably reliably be considered to echo or relate to a specific theme put forward by a person or group during the Campaign and those that could not be so connected. The specific themes included, for example, the disputes about the likely effect of continued Common Market membership on unemployment in Britain, on 'shopping-basket' prices, on the world role of Britain, on whether or not EEC trade or world trade mattered most, and so on.

45 At the first interviews with the Birmingham panel sample, three out of four 'had a go' at specifying the decisive factors as they saw them. One-quarter gave replies that were classified in Group I – direct effects on their everyday lives. These were mainly concerned with unemployment and cost of living prospects and only rarely with sovereignty. A similar number relied on what their friends did, or on their attitudes towards foreign entanglements (usually mistrust), or simply took the easy way out, and regarded membership as irrevocable. These are coded in Group IV. More abstract considerations received fewer nominations, a little under one-fifth mentioning 'political or defence arguments' (Group III) and only one-seventh general economic arguments such as trading opportunities and industrial expansion (Group II). The rest, in Group V, either did not vote, did not make up their minds, gave uncodable answers or – more often – gave no answer at all. Most people gave only *one* 'decisive factor' and those that gave more than one generally confined them to the same Group. About half of the decisive factors mentioned were allocated to one or other of the specific theme codes in Groups I, II and III. As has been said, these were codes that, it was hoped, represented the more prominent of the many arguments for staying in or pulling out of the Common Market that were later stressed in the campaign about to begin.

46 Though the Campaign coverage regularly and comprehensively brought the arguments of the pro- and anti-EEC factions to the attention of listeners and viewers, there were few changes in the replies of the panel sample between mid-April and mid-June. The prominence in the media coverage of arguments about employment prospects and about opportunities for industry may account for the modest increases in the fre-

quency with which these two factors were mentioned. There were similarly small rises in the mention of the arguments that 'membership of the EEC is a good way to avoid future wars' and that 'whatever the present prospects, international co-operation such as the EEC is right for the future'. These are issues that, from a somewhat cursory inspection of the transcripts of some of the major programmes, do *not* appear to have received much explicit coverage. An example of a point that *was* aired in several programmes but which did not 'register' with many people, it seems, was that 'trade with the EEC is falling, whilst with the rest of the world, it is rising'. However, support for almost all the factors was low, and the changes minimal.

47 In the third and fourth interviews, people were asked to say which, if any, of a number of recent broadcasts about the Referendum – 27 in all – they had seen or heard. The 'real deciding factors' specified by the inevitably rather small numbers who had seen each of five of these 27 broadcasts (those with the largest audiences amongst this panel sample) exhibited few differences from those given by the total sample. The largest differences were (a) viewers of Harold Wilson's *Talk-In* made comparatively frequent references (about 13% did so) to 'the opportunities for British industry in the EEC', (b) viewers of the Jenkins/Benn *Panorama* confrontation differed from others only in being more likely to mention the importance of EEC membership in avoiding future wars (14%), (c) this deciding factor was also given comparatively frequently by viewers of Harold Wilson's appearance in *Nationwide*, as was 'the prospects for shop prices' (11%). These differences – which it must be emphasised, may well be due to nothing more than chance – do not suggest that many people were noticeably swayed by what they saw or heard, at least in individual broadcasts. Such a direct and simple relationship between the message and the receivers' response is, of course, improbable, unless 'the receivers' have to make a decision on a subject on which they have almost totally blank minds and on which they are not subject to peer group or other influences.

48 In passing, it may be noted that the patterns of viewing of, and listening to, these 27 selected programmes give a neat example of selective exposure at work. The average number seen or heard was 5·3, made up of 2·1 out of 9 'pro-EEC' programmes (e.g. a pro-marketeer in *Nationwide* or a Referendum broadcast by Britain in Europe), 1·7 out of 7 'anti-EEC' programmes, and 1·5 out of 11 neutral programmes (e.g. *A Bus Round Europe* or the Oxford Union Debate). The great majority of both Yes

voters and No voters reported seeing or hearing roughly equal numbers of the pro- and anti-EEC broadcasts enquired about, but almost all the remainder of the Yes's said they saw more pro- than anti- programmes, whereas the remaining No's were fairly evenly split between those who saw more pro- than anti- broadcasts. It would seem that there may have been some deliberate avoidance of anti-EEC programmes by the Yes voters.

49 The deciding factors mentioned by the Yes and No voters naturally differed considerably, the Birmingham panel results revealing that the gap between the two groups increased substantially during the Campaign. Supporters of staying in the EEC changed little in their feelings about what 'the real deciding factors' were, only one – that being in the EEC was a good way of avoiding wars – gaining any significant support. Those favouring pulling out of the EEC, on the other hand, increasingly felt that a variety of specific effects on their everyday lives were the really important factors, to which they added increasing criticism of EEC policies and growing willingness to admit dislike of foreign entanglements.

50 Were these changes the results of exposure to the extensive coverage in the mass media? If so, then above-average media users should exhibit the changes whilst below-average media users should not. This did not happen. Where changes occurred, they tended to be common to both above- and below-average users. This absence of any substantial influence by the broadcasting coverage of the campaign on what people thought the decisive issues were was confirmed by the post-Referendum survey. Though many of the most frequent listeners to or viewers of campaign broadcasts said they had found the coverage helpful in explaining what the main 'pro' and 'anti' arguments were, their statements about what they saw as the 'real deciding factors' hardly differed at all from those given by people who neither listened to nor viewed any Referendum programmes. Moreover, they were no more likely than others to adduce specific, rather than unspecific, themes as being the deciding factors for them. They may have heard them propounded on radio and television and in the papers, but this was not enough to convince them, it seems, that these *were* the important issues. If frequent exposure to the broadcast coverage produced any effect at all, it seems likely that it was confined to a modest increase in the proportion of No voters specifying 'general political and defence arguments' – a rare category for the No's to choose.

51 The biggest influence on the mentioning of specific themes was the extent

to which people talked about the Referendum with their friends. Those who did *not* do so included only 22% who were specific in their nomination of the deciding factors, whereas amongst those who did, the corresponding figure was twice as high, 43%. It was in the ebb and flow of conversation, apparently, that the arguments became clearer and sharper.

Influencing Voting Decisions

52 Though 'helping me to make up my mind which way to vote' was less often endorsed than were the other four 'functions' of the Campaign coverage about which listeners and viewers were asked in the post-Referendum survey, nevertheless 38% *did* credit broadcasting with having made a contribution – even if only a small one. Many of these, it transpired, were people who had made up their minds long ago, the implication being that, for them, 'helpfulness' meant confirming them in their opinions. For quite a few others as well, it seems, 'helpfulness' meant reinforcing an existing inclination. Of those who claimed to have made up their minds during the Campaign *and* who found the broadcasting coverage helpful, more than half said that their feelings about which way they were going to vote did not change, more than a third said they *had* changed, the remainder (about one in ten) admitted that they had simply become more confused. Altogether, there were no more than about 5% of the total sample in whom 'conversion' occurred during the Campaign

Voting Decisions and Frequency of Referendum Programme Listening and Viewing

		Heard Radio progs.			*Saw Television progs.*		
	Total	*Several times a day*	*About once a day*	*Less often*	*Several times a day*	*About once a day*	*Less often*
	%	%	%	%	%	%	%
A. Didn't change	79	74	76	80	76	78	85
Became –							
more pro/less anti	9	12	10	8	10	9	6
more anti/less pro	4	3	5	4	4	5	3
more undecided	8	11	9	8	10	8	6
	100	100	100	100	100	100	100
B. Voted Yes	56	62	59	57	56	59	54
No	23	22	26	20	28	22	19
Didn't vote	18	15	11	19	14	16	22
Didn't say	3	1	4	3	2	3	4
	100	100	100	100	100	100	100

and who believed broadcasting to have been instrumental. The *direction* in which this change of heart took place was, for the few who changed, more often than not in favour of staying in the EEC rather than pulling out – and this is true of both frequent and infrequent listeners and viewers. As the table on page 57 shows, frequent listeners and viewers were, in their own estimation, a little more changeable than others, but on the day they turned out to be rather more likely than others to use their vote.

53 In the Birmingham sample, as in the national post-Referendum survey, below-average users of the media coverage tended to include fewer Yes voters, more No voters, and more 'undecided's', than did above-average users. This was so right from the beginning. The proportions of both Yes and No voters increased slightly as the Campaign progressed, at the expense of the 'undecided's', the increase being a little greater in the case of the No's. If heavy consumption of the media coverage had influenced voting in one direction or another, the heavier users should have shown bigger trends than the light users, but this is not so. The media coverage might, of course, have influenced voting in *both* directions, analysis of the *changes* of intention being necessary to disclose this. As has been said, two-thirds of the panel sample both knew in mid-April which way they intended to vote and in fact carried out their intention on 5 June. A few (8%), however, *did* change their minds during the Campaign and a larger proportion (16%) made up their minds and voted, having originally been undecided. Though these numbers are small, it appears that – if anything – it was the above-average media users who were more likely to change sides, and the below-average media users who made up their minds.

54 It has sometimes been suggested that an awareness of which way the vote is likely to go – derived mainly from the opinion polls – is likely to influence voting by having a 'band-wagon' effect. In the Referendum Campaign, slightly more than half the panel sample started by believing (correctly) that the Yes's would win, twice as many as believed that the vote would go the other way. The rest were unprepared to hazard a prediction. By the third interviews, a few days before the Referendum, only 13% still thought that the No's would win, nearly all the rest realising that they would be unlikely to do so. That this increased understanding of the situation must have derived directly or indirectly from the media is certain. However, as many below-average as above-average users of the media coverage became correctly informed on this point. This is, of course, an

example of the kind of information that could as easily be picked up by no more than casual listening or viewing of news bulletins, or reading of the headlines in the Press, as by avid following of special current affairs programmes about the Referendum. The only surprise is why *everybody* did not become aware that the vote would almost certainly favour the Yes's. The answer is almost certainly 'wishful thinking', virtually all those still believing that the No's would win being intending No voters.

55 But did the widespread conviction that the decision of the Referendum would be to stay in the EEC affect the voting? There is some evidence to suggest that it could have done. The small number of people who changed from believing that the No's would win to realising that the Yes's would probably do so swung towards the 'stay in' position whereas the non-changers stuck to their original voting intentions. This supports the idea of a band-wagon effect. However, much of the swing in voting intention had, in fact, occurred by the time of the *second* interviews, when, unfortunately, the question about the expected result of the Referendum was not asked. This removes any possibility of conclusively resolving the chicken-and-egg problem of whether changes in belief about the likely winner preceded or followed changes in voting intention.

56 It has often been suggested that personal influence plays a more important role than do the mass media in communicating information and influencing decisions. The results of the present enquiry lend support to this view. Those who talked about the Referendum a lot with family or friends, (particularly the latter) differed markedly from the others in their ability to answer the questions about the EEC correctly and also – in some respects – in the kind of arguments that were decisive for them. But it was 'being in agreement' with one's family and friends rather than simply talking to them or not that was important when it came to decision-making. Those who were surrounded in their own homes by people who thought very differently found it difficult to maintain a definite line, it seems, and were inclined to 'waver'.

57 Other possibly influential factors considered in relation to deciding which way to vote were 'having close friends from Common Market countries (other than Eire)', 'political affiliation' and 'Trade Union membership'. Two of these three, 'having Common Market nationals as friends' and 'political party allegiance', *were* related to voting behaviour but Trade Union membership was not. However, political affiliation is closely

related to education and to socio-economic group and it seemed possible that the sort of associations disclosed were, in part at least, the expression of 'class' differences. This was confirmed by a deeper analysis of the data, which showed that, within the ranks of Labour and Conservative supporters, the voting patterns of the socio-economic groups were indeed different.

58 To conclude, the only factors associated at all closely with voting Yes or No, or not voting at all, were 'class', 'age', and 'talking to family and friends'. Listening to and viewing a lot of Referendum programmes, Party allegiance, and so on, were *not*. Admittedly, there *was* a modest relationship between 'not listening and viewing much' and 'not voting in the Referendum', but this can be presumed to be a reflection of a general lack of interest rather than evidence to support an hypothesis that broadcast programmes helped to persuade people to vote.

59 The processes whereby people came to their decisions about which way to vote were bound to be complex and individual, and in the case of the EEC Referendum had had a long time in which to develop. As has been seen, most had decided before the first interviews took place in April. All that this study could do was to confirm that simple hypotheses, such as that the broadcast and Press coverage of the Campaign directly influenced the outcome one way or another are implausible. Some arousal of interest may well have occurred, some information about the EEC may have been conveyed, but there is no support for the view that broadcasting either 'told people what to think' or even 'what to think about'.

2 Listeners' Opinions of the Experiment in Broadcasting Parliament

The experiment in broadcasting Parliament ran for four weeks, from 9 June to 4 July 1975, during which there were occasional live relays, but most coverage was in the form of recorded excerpts, used in television as well as radio programmes, and on Independent as well as BBC channels. Radio 4's *Today in Parliament* and *Yesterday in Parliament* were each doubled in length to 30 minutes (except on Saturday mornings) and consisted of recorded excerpts with linking commentary.

Two questionnaires were sent to the Listening Panel,* one before the experiment began and the other immediately after it. The first asked Panel members about their listening, viewing and newspaper reading of current affairs, their interest in politics, their listening to and opinion of the existing *Today in Parliament* and *Yesterday in Parliament,* and their interest in the projected broadcasts of the actual proceedings of Parliament. The second sought opinions of the experiment in retrospect, and of the experimental versions of *Today in Parliament* and *Yesterday in Parliament.* 1949 Panel members returned the first questionnaire, and 1799 the second questionnaire, with 1401 returning both. It is the latter that have been used in the analysis that follows.

Panel members were asked whether, before the experiment started, they thought the BBC would make a good job of broadcasting Parliament, and, after the event, whether they thought the BBC had, in fact, done so. Before the experiment started a very large majority (83%) said they expected good coverage, and on the whole these expectations were borne out. Those with little interest in politics were slightly less appreciative of the broadcasts than were those with keen interest, but even so very few of them (only 4%) were really critical of the BBC's performance.

Although about one in five of those who had expected thc BBC to make 'an extremely good job' of broadcasting Parliament recorded a somewhat less favourable opinion of the actual broadcasts, this was more than

* A sample of over 3000 listeners who report their reactions to selected radio programmes if they happen to hear them. See Methods and Services booklet, available from Audience Research Department.

compensated by the higher opinions expressed by those who had expected less good coverage, so that the overall proportion endorsing 'extremely good' was even higher for the actual broadcasts than it had been for expectations of them.

Proportion who thought the BBC did	%
an extremely good job	37
a good job	47
a moderate job	11
a poor job	1
a very poor job	–
No reply/didn't hear any	4
	100

Nearly three-fifths considered the time devoted to broadcasting Parliament during the experiment to have been 'about right', the remaining two-fifths being split equally between those who thought it too much and those who thought it too little. Younger listeners and – not surprisingly – those keenest on politics were, on balance, inclined to say that it had been too little. Older listeners and the politically uninterested thought it had been too much.

The programmes most affected by the experimental broadcasting of Parliament were *Today in Parliament* and *Yesterday in Parliament*. Audiences for the experimental programmes increased significantly, and then fell back again in the four weeks immediately after the experiment, when the programmes reverted to their fifteen-minute summary format. The reasons for listening or not listening to *Today in Parliament* and *Yesterday in Parliament* given by the Panel members who returned both questionnaires confirmed that a minority (of about one in twelve) had decided to listen *because* of the experiment. The majority of those who listened, however, had already been listeners before the experiment.

In view of the generally appreciative response to the experiment as a whole, it is a little surprising to find no improvement in the reaction to the experimental version of *Today in Parliament*, as indicated by the way in which Panel members rated it on seven 'dimensions' defined by pairs of adjectives or descriptive phrases, e.g. clear/confusing. In fact, it fell short of that for the fifteen-minute summary version in three respects, being thought less informative, more confusing and more 'scrappy'. The General Evaluation (derived from the dimension 'worth hearing/not worth hearing') for the experimental version was 80, compared with 81 for the summary version.

The explanation seems to be, not that listeners were unable to discriminate between the two versions, but that the rating scale format left many of them – those who gave the summary version top rating – with no scope for registering improvement. This was borne out by a closer look at the General Evaluation 'worth hearing/not worth hearing' scale, which showed that, of those who gave the summary version top rating, as many as 67% nevertheless said that they preferred the experimental version. It could also be argued that 'well worth hearing', with its implication of utilitarian listening and objective evaluation, was too insensitive a form of words for comparing responses to these programmes. Indeed, the selection of word pairs for the Reaction rating scales may inadvertently have been somewhat unfair to the experimental version, in that they tended to focus on the strong points of the summary version. However, it is quite clear that a not inconsiderable minority of listeners to the experimental programmes were somewhat less impressed by them than they had been by the earlier programmes, and that they balanced out those who favoured the new version.

When asked to state their preferences between the experimental and summary forms in respect of certain specific criteria (most of which are,

Preferences for Experimental and Summary Versions in Performing Specific 'Functions' for Listeners

	Prefer experimental version %	*Prefer summary version* %	*Both equally satisfactory* %	*Both equally unsatisfactory* %	*no opinion* %	*Total* %
For helping you form your own opinion of the politicians concerned	79	5	11	2	3	100
For stimulating your interest	69	14	13	2	2	100
For enjoyable listening	59	19	14	3	5	100
For holding your attention	59	19	18	2	2	100
For helping you form your own opinion of political issues	47	15	28	4	6	100
For providing the sort of information you want	49	26	22	1	2	100
For being the right length	43	31	19	3	4	100
For giving the right amount of detail	33	30	30	4	3	100
For impartiality	28	17	50	1	4	100
For clarity	29	36	33	1	1	100
For neatly summing up the main points of the day's proceedings in Parliament	25	45	28	1	1	100

in a sense, 'functions' of the broadcasts for their listeners) it became apparent that the experimental version did, indeed, lead on those criteria which were *not* covered in the Reaction rating scales. Above all, the experimental version was preferred for 'helping you to form your own opinion of politicians' and for 'stimulating your interest'. In contrast, the summary version was most often preferred for 'neatly summing up the main points of the day's proceedings', for 'clarity', for 'being the right length' and for 'giving the right amount of detail'.

What, if anything, did listeners to *Today in Parliament* think was gained by broadcasting excerpts from Parliament instead of having just a summary? By far the most frequent reply was that the illustrated programmes generated a sense of 'immediacy' or 'involvement'. Parliament became less 'remote' and more 'important'. The 'authentic' experience of Parliament in session was more interesting and had much more 'atmosphere' than 'second-hand' summaries, however competent those summaries might be. Some said the experimental programmes were simply livelier, more fun to hear, at times even amusing: but many seemed to feel it went deeper than that. They were discovering a sharper and more 'personal' awareness of Parliament and political issues. Other points raised by listeners were:

'The direct relaying of MP's own words removed any question of misquotation and reduced the possibility of "editorial bias".'

'The nuances of emphasis, phrasing, degree of feeling in the voice, etc., made up a fairly important part of the meaning of any spoken statement, and this part of the meaning was now getting through. It was observed that even the best of newsreaders might sometimes get the emphasis wrong – and no newsreader could reproduce the original speaker's voice with its partly involuntary clues about his character and mood.'

'You get to know the people more – and begin to understand the procedure. I thought there was good drama – and good laughs. The contrasts between bad behaviour and serious debates were sharper than I expected.'

'You know you are hearing the unbiased truth of what is said. You can also judge how a speaker performed and form a better opinion of him – e.g. you might disagree with what he is saying but be impressed by the manner in which he argues his point.'

'It gives an immediacy and an importance to proceedings that one is tempted to take for granted. It makes it believable.'

'One can gauge the personality and sometimes even the honesty of the speaker, and his grip on his subject-matter – still more when he is being heckled.'

'With all its stumbling and bumbling, rubbish and rhetoric, sense and nonsense, this is authentic.'

'I felt I was amongst them and that I would take more interest in what goes on if this was a regular broadcast.'

'Not a great deal (was gained). I feel I would rather have the bare facts rather than having to listen to a lot of Parliamentary waffle to get the gist of an argument or point of view.'

As was to be expected, most (about two-thirds) of those who completed both questionnaires agreed that during the experiment they felt they were being better informed about the matters currently under discussion in Parliament, and much the same proportion felt they had been made more interested in what was going on there. The only surprise was that as many as one-third did *not* feel any better informed. It might be expected that these would mainly be people who did not see or hear many of the broadcasts concerned, but this proved not to be the case. Only two out of every five of them had heard few of the broadcasts from Parliament; the rest simply did not, it seems, find them any more informative than the parliamentary reporting without recordings from the Chamber. The same picture emerged in the answers to a question about listeners' feelings of clarity about the rules and etiquette of the House of Commons. The majority (57%) said that after the experiment they felt clearer on these matters, but the large minority who did *not* make this reply proved not to consist solely or even mainly of people who had heard few of the broadcasts.

In the first of the two questionnaires sent to them, Panel members were asked whether they agreed or disagreed with twenty-six points of view about politicians and politics. Their answers clearly indicated that most of them viewed politicians with reserve. MPs were not usually expected to be 'among the ablest men and women in the country' nor to be 'brilliant in their speeches', neither were they seen as first and foremost altruistically concerned with society or the needs of their own constituents, whilst very few of those replying felt they could 'safely believe what politicians say'. In the second questionnaire Panel members were asked whether their opinion of politicians had altered in any way as a result of hearing them speaking in the House. They were not offered any ready-made alternative answers. About two-fifths made comments which suggested that there had been *some* modification of their opinion or understanding of politicians, but this was not always a simple uprating or downrating. The most frequent *welcome* modification was an improved ability to appreciate MPs as individuals. Hearing them speak in the Commons made them more interesting, easier to differentiate and more 'human', showing up their individual merits and deficiencies. The impression they derived from these broadcasts was occasionally quite different from the previous 'media image' of an individual politician, some said. Another direction in which change was noted as a result of the broadcasts was in a realisation by some people of how *difficult* it was to make a successful contribution in the House of Commons. The attitude of other Members meant that the speaker needed a sharp mind, sound information at his fingertips, and a good deal of courage, it was said.

Most *adverse* comment seemed to be concerned with manners. Some respondents apparently could not accept the 'schoolboyish' outbreaks of noise or the 'rudeness' of attacking speeches, and in only a few cases was the 'childish' element of Parliamentary behaviour viewed with sympathy, indulgence or unconcern.

Those whose opinion of politicians was low before the experiment tended to claim that this opinion had been confirmed or had deteriorated further, whereas those who initially regarded politicians favourably seldom indicated any loss of respect for them as a result of hearing these broadcasts.

Modification of Listeners' Opinions of Politicians

		Pre-experiment opinion of Politicians					
	All	*Very low*	*Low*	*Rather low*	*Not very high*	*High*	*Very high*
	%	%	%	%	%	%	%
Opinion raised	6	3	4	4	6	11	15
Ambivalent Direction not stated Modified in a way that does not imply raising or lowering	13	6	9	17	14	17	18
Opinion lowered	22	38	31	18	18	11	10
Opinion unchanged or confirmed	44	39	43	44	46	45	48
No reply	15	14	13	17	16	16	9
	100	100	100	100	100	100	100

Should the BBC continue to broadcast Parliament? According to the Panel members who completed these questionnaires, the answer was decisively 'Yes', 75% agreeing that the broadcasts should continue. The proportion taking this view was higher still amongst those who were keenest on politics, but even amongst those with scarcely a flicker of interest in politics the weight of opinion was in favour of continuation.

3 The Image of *Play for Today*

The main question to which this research addressed itself is 'How do viewers regard *Play for Today*? Do they see any common features in the plays shown under this title, and, if so, is there evidence of the title having acquired an unintended "image"?' In fact, *Play for Today* is the main outlet on BBC television for new 'full-length' plays. Beyond that, there is no intention of specialising in any particular genre or subject area. The title is not even intended to prescribe plays *for today* in the sense of being 'topical' or reflecting current preoccupations – a new play set squarely in the past would not be disqualified. However, plays which are not set in the present day or near it have been exceptional.

The Audience Research Department commissioned an opinion research agency, R.S.G.B., to administer a short interview (as part of an Omnibus Survey) to 2267 adults (minimum age 16) between 19 and 25 May. (Details of sampling and weighting procedures can be obtained from the R.S.G.B. report – RSGB/6505: *Play for Today Study*.) At the same time, viewer reaction to the group of six new *Play for Today* productions then in progress (Weeks 17–22) was explored by sending a brief questionnaire about each play to the Viewing Panel.

About half of the people interviewed by R.S.G.B. – slightly more among the younger age-groups and the 'upper' socio-economic groups – claimed to view *Play for Today* at least occasionally. 7% viewed it 'regularly'. This agrees closely with Audience Research's daily Survey estimates, for the six weeks preceding the R.S.G.B. interviews, of an average audience of four million viewers (8% of the United Kingdom population aged 5 and over).

Those who claimed to watch *Play for Today* either 'regularly' or 'occasionally' were asked to say in their own words whether, on the whole, they were satisfied with the plays. 53% were generally satisfied or 'liked the plays', 11% answered rather equivocally and 17% were not satisfied or 'did not like the plays'. The remaining 19% made no reply.

Non-viewers of the plays, as well as viewers, were asked to select from a list the phrases 'which best describe the plays you are likely to see on

Play for Today'. (They were handed a card bearing the list, and could choose as many or as few as they wished of the seventeen alternatives.)

The *Play for Today* viewers answered more freely than did non-viewers (the percentages choosing each statement tending to be higher), but if the statements are ranked from the most often to the least often selected, the order turns out to be markedly similar for both groups. In other words, if *Play for Today* has an 'image' among non-viewers which is based on hear-say or interpretation of the title, it is virtually indistinguishable from the viewing audience's conception backed by experience of the plays.

	Frequency of Endorsement	
	Viewers %	*Non-viewers* %
Statements:		
Plays which are true to life	42	32
which leave you feeling they were worth watching	35	24
which make you want to watch until the end	35	27
which give you something to think about	33	20
with a message about current social problems	31	17
which keep you happily entertained	28	27
which don't have a proper ending	23	10
which leave you feeling you haven't understood them	21	11
which are so varied that you don't know what to expect	20	15
about people you can sympathise with	18	11
which you just can't get into	17	14
with a lot of talking and not a lot of action	14	10
with too much sex	13	9
which you would consider unfit for family viewing	12	6
by famous writers of the past	12	11
by present-day writers, but set in the past	10	8
which leave you feeling depressed	8	5

Amongst the few noteworthy differences between viewers and non-viewers was the frequency of endorsement of 'Plays which keep you happily entertained'. This came second for non-viewers and sixth for viewers. Perhaps the phrase struck non-viewers as a safe choice on account on its complimentary tone and its vagueness compared with most of the alternatives. Apart from this, the most widely endorsed descriptions by both groups were 'plays which are true to life', 'which leave you feeling they were worth watching', 'which give you something to think about', and 'with a message about current social problems'. Coupled with the fact that no more than 18% of viewers and 11% of non-viewers selected 'plays about people you can sympathise with', this leads to an 'image' of serious, realistic plays which tend to be viewed thoughtfully, with interest, but on the whole detachedly.

As to the 'negative' side, the most frequently selected statements were 'plays which don't have a proper ending', 'plays which leave you feeling you haven't understood them' and 'plays which you just can't get into' (the last ranking higher, naturally enough, with non-viewers than with viewers). Smaller proportions chose 'plays with too much sex' and 'plays which you would consider unfit for family viewing', and very few 'plays which leave you feeling depressed'. This suggests that, when these plays fail to please, it is more likely to be because there is insufficient communication than because something that *did* get through proved unwelcome.

Of a list of ten reasons for not viewing *Play for Today*, the ones most frequently chosen by those who don't watch the series were: 'I can't watch TV at this time', 'I prefer another programme at this time', and 'I simply never get round to it'. Those reasons expressing antipathy – 'I don't like any television plays' and '*Play for Today* isn't my kind of play' – were chosen comparatively seldom, by 14% and 13% respectively. However, it is quite likely that some who selected the first set of reasons were simply finding an easy way out without having to appear to be critical.

The 'image' of *Play for Today* agreed pretty closely with the 'reality', as indicated by viewers' reactions to the six plays transmitted in May/June 1975. They included one clear 'success' *The Saturday Party*, and an equally clear 'failure' *Brassneck*. In *The Saturday Party* a stockbroker who has just lost his job is faced with drastic changes in his life-style and relationships, but the 'show goes on' in the form of a lavish Christmas party. It seems to have presented what was felt to have been a serious and 'topical' theme in a highly entertaining form. Viewers appear to have felt a kind of sympathy with and understanding of the characters which seemed lacking in the other plays. *Child of Hope*, based on Joel Carson's account of the trial of 37 Namibians under South African law, also aroused sympathy, but that seems to have been an impersonal feeling more concerned with the outrageous treatment of human beings by other human beings than with individuals.

By contrast, *Brassneck* seldom struck any chord of interest, sympathy or comprehension. This fierce attack on dishonesty in public life left most viewers 'cold', and was so 'nasty' that it antagonised a minority against the people responsible for the play, rather than against its target. It also disappointed some viewers who seemed ready to appreciate its intention by presenting too many facets of its subject and, perhaps, by omitting to provide even one attractive character.

Response to the remaining three plays was much less clear-cut. *The Dandelion Clock*, in which a Belfast child spends the day neurotically searching for her father, might have been expected to produce much sympathy and indignation, but did not. Apparently the dialect was an obstacle; so, perhaps, was the 'odd' behaviour of overwrought people. However, a substantial minority were impressed by this play.

Wednesday Love was a little better received. The story concerned a bored Manchester wife who falls in love with a student she meets in a drinking club. Eventually she leaves her family to pursue this chancy relationship. It was an example of what might be called an 'unprettified' play about personal relationships, which generally came near the middle of the scale between general enjoyment and general dislike.

In *The Floater* all parties agree that it is simpler and more satisfactory to convict a drug addict who is technically not guilty of the charge of peddling. It was advertised as a 'comedy' (as was *Brassneck*), and some viewers who expected a 'comedy' to provide a laugh a minute were aggrieved. Others seemed to disapprove of a 'serious matter' – an unjust trial – being treated humorously. Like most of the plays, this was viewed detachedly by most of the Panel Members who saw it, and some found it boring.

The Viewing Panel provided very little comment which could be clearly identified as 'expectations' based on experience, reputation, or the title *Play for Today*, as distinct from their hopes or requirements. What evidence there was suggested expectations of 'true to life' situations; themes and situations 'of our time' ('topical'; 'up-to-date'; 'real problems of today'); social comment; seriousness ('something to say'; 'thought-provoking'; 'depth' in characterisation). There was also some support for the view that 'one didn't know what to expect' – except it would probably be 'something different'.

These reactions make abundantly clear that viewers found in these *Plays for Today* very much what they expected to find – something worthwhile viewing, about real problems, giving them something to think about, but not often about characters they could sympathise with. They might not always like or enjoy what they saw but, except when misled into looking for 'traditional' comedy, they were not, it seems, surprised by the type of content.

4 What *The Changing Face of Medicine* Conveyed to its Viewers

Introduction

The Changing Face of Medicine was a series of three 50-minute documentaries broadcast on BBC1 on successive Thursdays during November 1975.

The first, 'Victories', looked at some of the ways in which medicine has changed over the last 15–20 years. It used excerpts from the first *Your Life in Their Hands* series to illustrate the advances that had been made in areas such as polio, heart disease, and Parkinson's disease, and also looked at new medical instruments such as the EMI-scanner which produces X-rays of the body in cross-section. As well as talking about the successes and the advances during this period, the programme also discussed some of the practical and ethical problems that had accompanied these advances, the limitations of medical treatment, and the fallibility of doctors.

The second programme, 'Mysteries', concerned some of the diseases which are still 'medical mysteries', and for which the causes and cures are still unknown. After looking briefly at schizophrenia and multiple sclerosis, the programme turned to the US National Cancer Programme, and concentrated on three aspects of the research being carried out within this Programme – viruses as a cause of cancer, the treatment of cancer with radiation and the treatment of cancer with drugs. There was some criticism of the political motivations of those involved in setting up the National Cancer Programme, and doubts were raised as to whether the large sums of money poured into the campaign could in fact do anything to speed the discovery of a cure.

In 'Prophecies', the final programme, viewers were asked to imagine that they were in the year AD 2000 and watching a documentary about current medical practices. The programme covered family planning and popuia-tion control, detection of congenital disorders, prevention of cancer, cures for kidney disease and for incontinence, and treatment for the mentally ill and for geriatrics. It depicted a health service in which the Government exercised considerable control, and in which national and individual health-hazards could be accurately predicated by the constant review of medical records at a central computer bank.

A research project was undertaken to determine the extent to which each of the programmes (*a*) increased viewers' knowledge and understanding of the causes, symptoms and methods of treatment of various illnesses, (*b*) aroused feelings of anxiety or depression, (*c*) affected viewers' attitudes towards medical research and the medical profession, or (*d*) proved to be in any way misleading. During the two days after each programme had been broadcast, some 150 members of the public who had watched the programme, and a similar number who had not watched it, completed detailed questionnaires which were designed to obtain information about their reactions to the programme and the immediate effects of the programme on their knowledge of, and attitudes towards, various medical topics.

To isolate any more *lasting* changes of attitude for which the programmes could have been responsible, a brief questionnaire was sent to a sample of some 2000 people throughout the country three weeks before the *Changing Face of Medicine* series began and a second questionnaire, covering much of the same ground as the first, three weeks after the series had ended. Some had watched the programme during the intervening period while others had not.

A brief postal questionnaire was also sent to a sample of some 2275 General Practitioners throughout the country a few weeks after the *Changing Face of Medicine* series had ended, with a view to examining their general attitudes towards television programmes dealing with medical topics, their reactions to the *Changing Face of Medicine* programmes and the effects of the programmes on their patients.

Programme 1: 'Victories'

The great majority of the comments made by viewers about 'Victories' were highly favourable. Most of them felt that the programme had been very good, very interesting and very informative, and there were no major criticisms. In addition, three-fifths indicated that, for them, the programme had contained just the right amount of detail while most of the rest felt that it was not detailed enough. Only 13% rated it 'difficult to understand'.

Early in the questioning (before it became apparent that the *Changing Face of Medicine* series was the main area of interest), people were asked whether they had seen anything on television recently that had made them feel squeamish. Three out of five viewers and a similar proportion of non-viewers could think of nothing and the remainder mostly claimed to have felt squeamish about scenes of violence in various programmes.

When asked to indicate how they had felt after seeing the programme, only a small minority claimed that the programme had left them feeling in any way *unhappy*, *worried*, *afraid* or *depressed*. The great majority indicated that they were left feeling *happy* and *reassured*, or that the programme had not affected their mood at all. Viewers who were particularly concerned about their health were the least likely to feel worried or depressed and the most likely to feel cheerful and reassured after the programme had ended.

People participating in the research were asked a number of 'general knowledge' questions about medical topics, some of which were dealt with in the programme while others were not. Those who had watched the programme proved to be somewhat more knowledgeable than those who had not watched it about medical topics in general, as evidenced by the fact that they were, on the whole, slightly more likely to give the correct answers to questions *not* covered in the programme. However, the fact that they were *considerably* more knowledgeable about many of the topics that *were* covered in the programme demonstrates that some points 'got across' to considerable numbers.

	Proportion giving correct answers	
	Viewers	*A similar group of non-viewers*
	%	%
Topics covered in 'Victories' –		
Treatment to prevent jaundice in babies born to mothers with incompatible rhesus factor in their blood	59	16
Purpose of EMI-scanner	75	47
Purpose of heart-lung machine	75	50
Treatment for narrowed heart valve	80	58
Importance of immunisation against polio	83	69
Description of artificial kidney	87	75
Treatment for Parkinson's disease	61	59
Topics not covered in 'Victories' –		
Treatment for overactive thyroid	70	58
Method of giving insulin to diabetics	91	82
Treatment for blockage of the liver due to cirrhosis	30	27

Only in one area was there any indication that some people who watched the programme might have been misled by what they had seen –

30% of those who had watched the programme believed, incorrectly, that the most usual treatment for Parkinson's disease was brain surgery, despite the fact that the programme had explained that earlier attempts to treat this disease with brain surgery had been only moderately successful, and that treatment with drugs was proving far more effective. Only 6% of non-viewers gave this incorrect reply.

Viewing 'Victories' seems to have had a limited effect on certain specific attitudes and beliefs. Those who saw the programme were far more conscious than were non-viewers of the continued importance of immunisation against polio. They were also less likely than those who did not see the programme to believe in the importance of specialised hospital care and treatment for people recovering from heart attacks. However, those who saw the programme were no more and no less worried than those who did not see the programme at the thought of having most of a list of illnesses that they were asked about, an exception being that more viewers than non-viewers were worried at the thought of having Parkinson's disease. Viewers and non-viewers were also very much alike in their opinions on the amount of progress they felt had been made in the treatment of most of the illnesses listed, whether the illness was mentioned in the programme or not. In view of this, it is not surprising that viewers and non-viewers were equally confident of the successful outcome of their treatment should they be suffering from these illnesses.

One unexpected result was that viewers appeared to have more faith in doctors than did non-viewers. And, despite the arguments put forward in the programme, they were somewhat *less* likely than those who did not see the programme to feel that 'advances in medical research bring with them almost as many problems as they solve'.

	Viewers %	*Non-viewers* %
'Medical advances bring about as many problems as they solve'		
Agree	43	53
Disagree	34	21
Undecided	23	26
	100	100

Programme 2: 'Mysteries'

'Mysteries' was almost as well regarded as was 'Victories', except for the criticism that it concentrated too much on research being carried out in the USA, and should have given more information about what was being done in Britain to find a cure for cancer.

The majority of its viewers claimed either that it had had no effect on their mood or that it had left them feeling mildly confident and reassured. However, the minority claiming that the programme had left them feeling worried or afraid was higher than for 'Victories', and there were slight indications that it was those viewers who were particularly concerned about their health, and those with a high general level of anxiety, who were the most likely to feel worried or afraid after seeing the programme.

Some examples of the extent to which certain facts were conveyed by the programme are given by the following figures.

	Proportion giving correct answers	
	Viewers	*A similar group of non-viewers*
	%	%
Type of women most susceptible to breast cancer	49	19
Effect of multiple sclerosis	92	78
Type of cancer which has been most successfully treated with drugs	60	48
Definition of schizophrenia	92	81
Type of people in whom leukaemia has most successfully been treated	83	74
Cure for schizophrenia	33	24
Cause of multiple sclerosis	70	65
Occasions when surgery unlikely to succeed in curing cancer	87	83
Cause of cancer	39	38
Main method of treatment for cancer	48	51

Viewers, and particularly female viewers under the age of 50, became considerably more aware of a few facts, that 'childless women are more susceptible to breast cancer than women with children', but the programme did not appear to increase their awareness of many others, e.g. that 'surgery is the main method of treatment for cancer', or that 'the cause of multiple sclerosis is not known'. There was also evidence to suggest that the programme caused some confusion with regard to the main cause of cancer. Although it was stressed in the programme that most cancer is caused by substances in the environment, 42% of viewers believed that most cancer was caused by viruses, compared with only 24% of non-viewers who gave this reply.

Other differences between the attitudes of viewers and non-viewers were that the former were considerably less likely than the latter to believe that 'the possibility of finding a cure for cancer was directly dependent upon the amount of money available for cancer research', and a little more likely to be aware that 'advances in medical research still have a long way to go'. An important finding was that viewers of the programme were marginally *less* likely than were non-viewers to be worried at the thought of having the illnesses mentioned in the programme, despite being more conscious than were those who had not watched the programme of the lack of progress in recent years in the treatment of these 'mysteries'.

Programme 3: 'Prophecies'

'Prophecies' was greeted a little more warmly than was 'Mysteries' but not quite so warmly as 'Victories'. In most of its viewers' eyes, it was interesting and thought-provoking, but whereas a sizeable minority felt that the predictions made about the state of medical research in the year 2000 were quite believable and would probably prove to be accurate, a similar number regarded the programme as too exaggerated and far-fetched.

As with the other two programmes, the great majority of its viewers once again claimed that the programme had had no effect on their mood, the small proportion saying that they had felt at all worried or afraid after

	Proportion giving correct answer	
	Viewers	*A similar group of non-viewers*
	%	%
Whether fluoride lollipops are currently on sale	81	76
Usual treatment for kidney failure	73	73
Whether tests exist to determine likelihood of smokers developing lung cancer	57	57
Whether women who breast feed their children get higher family allowance	92	93
Whether a medicine exists to enable people to choose the sex of their children	84	87
Main cause of cancer	7	10
Cure for incontinence	16	21
Chances of reversing female sterilisation operation	67	73
Whether life insurance premiums are always much higher for people who:		
(a) drink a lot	78	85
(b) smoke a lot	70	80

seeing it being somewhat higher than for 'Victories' and about the same as for 'Mysteries'.

Answers to a number of questions about the present position on some of the topics dealt with in the programme indicate that most of those who watched it had little difficulty in distinguishing future predictions from the current state of affairs. (See table p. 77.)

As will be seen, apart from the fact that the viewers were marginally more likely than the non-viewers to believe that 'life insurance premiums are always much higher nowadays for people who smoke or drink a lot', and slightly more optimistic about the chances of 'successfully reversing a female sterilisation operation', there is no real evidence to suggest that viewers had been in any way confused or misled by what they had seen.

People who had watched 'Prophecies' were very similar to those who had not watched it in their attitudes towards medical research and the medical profession in general, even in areas where the programme might have been expected to bring about changes in attitudes. They were no more likely to agree that 'The Government should not be allowed to interfere in matters concerning people's health', that 'There will be just as much illness around in 25 years' time as there is today' or that 'During the next 25 years there are likely to be great improvements in the way medical services are organised in this country'. They *were*, however, slightly more likely than non-viewers to believe that it was possible for 'experts to make accurate predictions about progress in medical research during the next 25 years'.

Again, as with the two earlier programmes, there was no evidence to suggest that viewers of 'Prophecies' were any more or any less worried than non-viewers at the thought of having any of the illnesses mentioned in the programme. Nor were they any more or less confident than non-viewers that the illnesses mentioned in the programme could be treated successfully.

Lasting Effects of Viewing the Programmes

This section is concerned with the findings of the two-stage postal survey, which would, it was hoped, give some indication as to whether or not the *Changing Face of Medicine* series had had any lasting effects on its viewers (at least in the few areas which it was possible to deal with in a brief questionnaire).

It was realised, of course, that there were any number of factors that could have brought about changes in people's attitudes during the period between completion of the two questionnaires (notably, a pay dispute amongst junior doctors), but it was hoped that by comparing shifts in the attitudes of viewers and of non-viewers of the series it would be possible to identify some changes for which the programmes could have been responsible. (One potentially important factor was the broadcasting of the play *Through the Night*, shortly after the *Changing Face of Medicine* series had ended. It concerned a woman who was admitted to hospital after discovering a lump on her breast, and her subsequent unfortunate experiences of inadequacies in the hospital service. To avoid any contamination of the results from this source, viewers of *Through the Night* were excluded from the analysis.)

The first difference observed was a slight fall in the proportions who said they worried about 'illness in general' during the period between the administration of the two questionnaires, but since the fall was common to both viewers and non-viewers of the programmes, it seems unlikely that the *Changing Face of Medicine* had anything to do with it. However, there were also modest *increases* in the proportions worrying specifically about cancer and about physical disability, and these increases were greater amongst those who had seen the programmes than amongst those who had not. The series may, therefore, have played some part in bringing them about. The magnitude of the swings was, however, quite small, and may well be due to nothing more than chance.

	Viewers %	*Non-viewers* %
Between answering first and second questionnaires:		
became *more* concerned about cancer	29	24
remained unchanged	64	63
became *less* concerned about cancer	7	13
	100	100
became *more* concerned about physical disability	24	21
remained unchanged	64	61
became *less* concerned about physical disability	12	18
	100	100

While approximately two out of five informants who had *not* seen the *Changing Face of Medicine* series showed some change in their attitudes towards medical research and the medical profession during the period between the administration of two questionnaires, the changes largely cancelled one another out. This was also true of *viewers* of the programmes in most respects, but it appears that the series may have made a few of them more likely to believe that 'doctors can successfully treat most illnesses nowadays', whilst at the same time increasing their belief that 'advances in medical research still have a long way to go'. The only other point that seems to have made a lasting impression, again on a small number, was that 'medical advances bring almost as many problems as they solve'. This, it will be recalled, did *not* emerge as one of the findings when the impact of 'Victories' – the programme in which the point was made most explicitly – was studied shortly after it was transmitted. This could, perhaps, be an example of a point of view that is noted at the time but the truth of which is only apprehended fully in the light of subsequent events. On the other hand, the before/after differences were so small that they may well be nothing more than chance fluctuations.

The Views of General Practitioners

Of the 2275 General Practitioners to whom a brief postal questionnaire was sent, 1639 (72%) replied, including 649 (40%) who had watched at least part of one or other of the *Changing Face of Medicine* programmes.

Seven out of ten were in favour of having documentary programmes dealing with medical matters on television, just under two out of ten being opposed to such programmes, while the remainder were undecided. The main criticisms of those opposed to medical documentaries on TV were of 'sensationalism' and of 'exploiting differences of opinion between experts for the sake of good television'.

As to the *Changing Face of Medicine* programmes themselves, 'Victories' was considered the most suitable for general viewing and 'Mysteries' the least suitable; though even for 'Mysteries' the great majority agreed that most of it had been suitable. The doctors also believed that the programmes had given a fair representation of the progress of medical research over the last 15 years, 87% choosing the alternative answers 'very fair' or 'quite fair' for 'Victories' and 72% doing so for 'Mysteries'.

No more than one-fifth of the doctors claimed that any of their patients had mentioned the *Changing Face of Medicine* programmes and of these, more than half said that their patients had simply mentioned the programmes in passing. Only 6% said that patients had thought they might be suffering from one of the conditions mentioned in the programmes, and none claimed that there had been any increase in the numbers attending their surgeries as a result of the programmes.

When doctors were asked whether they felt that those patients who *had* mentioned the programmes had been worried or reassured by what they had seen, they proved to be roughly equally divided in their opinions. However, the answers they gave were strongly related to their personal attitudes towards medical programmes on television. Amongst those who were opposed to such programmes, 68% felt that their patients had been worried and 6% that they had been reassured, compared with 26% and 31% respectively amongst doctors who were in favour of such programmes. How far the answers given were based on objective observations and how far on subjective attitudes must, in the light of these findings, remain an open question.

The final question asked doctors to say whether or not those patients who *did* mention the programmes seemed to have been misled by what they had seen. One in six of the minority whose patients had mentioned the programmes reported that this had occurred.

Some felt that patients had misinterpreted specific scenes or sentences (no particular scene was mentioned more than once or twice), while others claimed that as a result of seeing the programmes some patients had become over-optimistic about medical treatment, and more inclined to believe that medical technology held the answers to all their problems. In addition, a handful of patients had, they reported, confused fantasy with reality, and believed that all or part of 'Prophecies' had been referring to present-day medicine.

5 'Daily Life in the 1970s'

A question of considerable importance when planning radio and television series is 'How many, and what kind of, people are normally available to listen or to view at different times of day?' Audience Research has sought to answer this question several times throughout its existence, starting as early as 1938 (when one finding – that most people had finished their evening meal before 7.00 p.m. – proved quite an eye-opener, it seems!). The biggest exercise of this kind came in 1961, when a large and representative sample of people kept records of their activities for a week in specially-prepared 'diaries'. This led to the preparation of a widely consulted document 'The People's Activities' (subsequently published by BBC Publications), which showed – in a lengthy series of charts and tables – what people of different kinds were doing half-hour by half-hour, on weekdays, on Saturdays and on Sundays.

This information has now been brought up to date, by means of *two* similar surveys, one in the late summer of 1974 and the other in February 1975, so that seasonal variations could be explored. The range of information collected was also expanded, by giving people the opportunity of recording secondary as well as main activities, whilst the lower age limit was dropped from 16 down to 5, the information in the case of young children being obtained from the parents. Most of the analysis has now been completed, but only preliminary reports on the two enquiries have as yet been issued. A comprehensive report giving the results of both enquiries, together with a commentary on the findings, is being prepared for publication but the earliest that it is likely to appear is mid-1977.

Extracts from two of the 'half-hour tables' from the preliminary reports will be found overleaf. They show, inter alia, that as early as 6.00–6.30 p.m. on weekdays 'viewing TV' as a main activity has already become the largest single category of activity, occupying 25% of the population. Many more are viewing as a *secondary* activity. 'Eating a meal' comes next (22%), with 'domestic duties' third (17%). 10% are still at work and 9% are otherwise 'not at home'. Differences between the behaviour of sub-groups of the population follow familiar and expected patterns. Turning to the second chart, for 10.00–10.30 a.m. on Sundays, the most striking figure is the very high proportion of 15–24-year-olds in bed, 40%!

What people are doing between 6.00 and 6.30 p.m. on Weekdays

	Total	*Age*					*Sex*	
		5–14	*15–24*	*25–44*	*45–64*	*65+*	*M*	*F*
	%	%	%	%	%	%	%	%
Main Activity:								
Listening to radio	1	–	–	–	1	2	1	–
Watching television	25	27	19	18	25	51	29	21
Personal care and meals	23	22	28	22	24	16	22	23
Work and school time	10	4	13	15	10	3	15	5
Domestic duties	17	4	17	28	20	8	7	25
Other at home type activities	14	23	11	10	14	11	15	13
Not at home – indoor activities	7	15	7	3	3	7	6	7
Not at home – outdoor activities	2	3	3	2	1	1	2	2
Asleep or in bed	1	–	1	1	1	1	1	–
No information	1	3	1	1	1	2	1	1
	100	100	100	100	100	100	100	100

What people are doing between 10.00 and 10.30 a.m. on Sundays

	Total	*Age*					*Sex*	
		5–14	*15–24*	*25–44*	*45–64*	*65+*	*M*	*F*
	%	%	%	%	%	%	%	%
Main Activity:								
Listening to radio	2	3	2	2	1	4	3	2
Watching television	1	–	–	–	1	3	1	–
Personal care and meals	23	28	22	21	24	15	22	24
Work and school time	4	1	4	6	5	*	7	1
Domestic duties	28	8	18	37	37	38	15	38
Other at home type activities	13	18	4	9	14	26	18	9
Not at home – indoor activities	7	19	3	3	4	5	7	7
Not at home – outdoor activities	6	7	6	6	6	3	8	4
Asleep or in bed	15	13	40	15	8	2	18	13
No information	2	3	–	1	1	3	2	1
	100	100	100	100	100	100	100	100

Comparison of the findings with those of 1961 is complicated by changes in the ways in which the activities have been coded or grouped. There seems little doubt, however, that people's daily behaviour patterns in the mid-70s differed little, in broad outline, from those of the early 1960s (which themselves clearly recalled findings a decade earlier). This can be seen from the following figures in which the 1961 and 1975 findings for a particular age group – the 25–44-year-olds – are given side by side for some selected half-hours on weekdays.

Activities of 25–44-year-olds

	6.30–7.00 a.m.		*8.00–8.30 a.m.*		*10.30–11.00 a.m.*		*1.00–1.30 p.m.*	
	1961	*1975*	*1961*	*1975*	*1961*	*1975*	*1961*	*1975*
	%	%	%	%	%	%	%	%
Main activities:								
Listening	1	–	–	1	1	–	2	–
Viewing	–	–	–	–	–	–	1	3
Meals/personal care	7	15	25	24	1	4	21	26
Bed	79	74	12	13	2	3	2	1
Other at home	2	3	23	27	28	29	22	24
Work	7	7	35	34	52	58	43	39
Other not at home	–	–	–	–	12	5	6	5
No information	4	1	5	1	4	1	3	2
	100	100	100	100	100	100	100	100

	5.30–6.00 p.m.		*7.30–8.00 p.m.*		*9.30–10.00 p.m.*		*11.00–11.30 p.m.*	
	1961	*1975*	*1961*	*1975*	*1961*	*1975*	*1961*	*1975*
	%	%	%	%	%	%	%	%
Main activities:								
Listening	2	–	2	–	3	–	1	–
Viewing	8	11	35	34	36	38	10	20
Meals/personal care	21	23	3	7	7	7	3	14
Bed	1	1	1	1	6	2	70	41
Other at home	28	37	32	32	25	24	8	12
Work	28	23	7	9	5	7	2	4
Other not at home	8	4	17	16	15	19	3	8
No information	4	1	3	1	3	3	3	1
	100	100	100	100	100	100	100	100

Getting-up times haven't changed much, it seems, and nor have meal-times, whilst the proportions at work during the day resemble one another closely. The biggest differences are (i) that fewer of these 25–44-year-olds are 'out' other than at work during the daytime, and (ii) that bed-times have moved a good half-hour or more later. There is no denying that both of these *could* be the result of lengthened television transmissions, non-workers (mainly housewives) now having regular daytime television programmes to watch if they wish, whilst the scheduling of programmes of wide appeal late at night is now more common than it used to be. However, this is only speculation. There could well be many other influences at work.